Addiction

The Parent's Journey From Hell To Hope

Mary Allyson

ISBN 978-1-0980-3460-3 (paperback)
ISBN 978-1-0980-3461-0 (hardcover)
ISBN 978-1-0980-3462-7 (digital)

Christian Faith Publishing, Inc.
832 Park Avenue
Meadville, PA 16335
www.christianfaithpublishing.com

Printed in the United States of America

To God, my creator and comforter.

To my wonderful husband, Guy, my best friend, and staunchest supporter during the writing process.

To my fabulous daughters, who are conquering addiction, living a sober life "one day at-a-time."

To my Mom and Dad, the most loving and caring parents a daughter could ask for.

To Mike Speakman, my mentor, founder of PAL (parents of addicted loved-ones).

To the PAL Board of Directors and PAL facilitators who give unselfishly of their time to help grow the PAL organization, educating and helping thousands of parents with broken hearts.

Contents

Preface

According to Elizabeth Kubler-Ross and her book *Death and Dying* (1969), there are six stages of grieving: denial, isolation, anger, bargaining, depression, and acceptance. It is my opinion that these stages parallel any type of loss a person may face during their lifetime, especially the circumstances a parent finds themselves while moving through the devastating perils of addiction with their adult son or daughter.

Finding out that you have a child with addiction issues/challenges is coming to the realization that you have suffered a loss; your child has been lost to a disease. You no longer recognize them. The disease has a stranglehold on their brain, causing them to be someone that is barely recognizable. Some parents feel it might be somewhat easier to deal with an actual death than watching their loved one slowly succumb to a life of desperation while slowly sinking into a state of hopelessness (see the introduction). Their brain is telling them that the only way to survive is to use again and again.

In the grief process, others have explained it as a ten-step process: shock, emotional release, physical symptoms, panic, guilt, hostility, inactivity, gradual recovery, and adjusting. Recognizing the various views on the stages of grief, I decided to use an eight-step grief process, with each chapter in this book representing a stage of grief for a parent with an addicted adult child:

> Denial: trying to avoid the "truth"
>
> Shock: facing the "truth"
>
> Release of Emotions: frustrated with the "truth"
>
> Guilt/bargaining: bartering with the "truth"
>
> Isolation/depression: when the "truth" hurts
>
> Education: understanding the "truth"
>
> Adjusting: focusing on the "truth"
>
> Acceptance: using the "truth" to move forward

For the most part, each of these chapters/stages in this book is a stage likened to the stages of grieving when a parent experiences the loss of their adult child to addiction. Eight of the nine chapters have specific questions for you to answer, a description/explanation, helping you realize and understand how a particular stage might pertain to you and the circumstances you may find yourself. Each question attempts to describe the various emotions/behaviors that parallel these eight stages of grief. The last chapter, chapter nine, discusses the twelve-step spiritual journey that addicts and family members may opt to follow in their own particular recovery process.

However, everyone's experience is one of a kind, making it difficult to generalize. I leave it to each of you to apply this material as it fits your unique situation and personality. Some of you parents may move through the stages slower/faster than others or perhaps bounce back and forth, depending on your own life experiences and attitudes. The principal goal in this book is to help parents keep moving forward, rather than stagnating, until they have reached a point that gives them understanding, peace, serenity, and a renewed sense of hope. Lastly, I'll use the Al-Anon slogan, "Take what you want and leave the rest."

Try to remember when facing this crisis that grief and loss are a normal and unavoidable part of life; and if you want to grow and learn from your loss, you need to address the negative patterns you have been taught and practiced in the past. You need to face and embrace your loss if you ever want to truly work through it and recover. In the case of your addicted loved one, you may ask why is it that you need to recover. After reading this book, you will come to understand why recovery is necessary for you, as well as your addicted child. With this, I leave you with this famous quote:

> You can't go back and change the begin-
> ning. But, you can start where you are and
> change the ending. (C. S. Lewis)

Introduction

A few weeks ago, my younger sister spotted an entry on Facebook titled "I Hope You Never." The page describes a parent's feelings about having an addicted child and then goes on to describe the addict's feelings about their addiction. The Facebook public page reads:

> If you are lucky enough to not understand addiction, then good for you.
>
> I hope you never have to.
>
> I hope you never see someone you love disappear before your eyes, while standing right in front of you.
>
> I hope you never have to lie awake all night praying the phone doesn't ring, yet hoping it does at the same time.
>
> I hope you never know the feeling of doing everything you thought was right and still watch everything go wrong.
>
> I hope you never love an addict."

"I hope you never live as an addict.

I hope you never know what it means to live afraid
of yourself.

To never trust yourself.

To fight a raging war inside your own mind every
moment.

To feel unwanted and unworthy.

To need something that you know is destroying
you and to do anything for it.

To trade yourself, your life, your soul and still end
up broken and alone.

To give away everything and everyone you had.

To have no answers. To always question. To have
no choice yet have to choose to fight your
battle.

I hope you never live as an addict.[1]

Is there hope in hell?

When I moved to Phoenix, Arizona, I learned about
a meeting at my church called PAL (parents of addicted
loved ones). Since I hadn't yet found an Al-Anon group,
I decided to give PAL a try. When I walked in the meeting room, the leader and founder, Mike Speakman, greeted
me with, "Welcome to hell," and a big smile. I was a little
shocked; but the more I thought about that statement, I

realized he had hit the nail on the head. That was the first and last time I heard him say it, but that statement has always stuck with me.

Those of us who have been through years of having a child dealing with addiction understand that statement. As believers, we experience battles of every kind. The enemy battles for our mind, wanting to fill it with fear, evil images, or guilt and worry. When we are rocked by bad news, it throws us into a tailspin, tearing down our spirit, driving us into the darkness where there is barely a glimmer of light.

No matter where you and your chemically dependent child find yourself in the addiction battle, keep in mind that people get better every day. While there is widespread pessimism about the possibility of a person changing, there are a lot of reasons to be hopeful. Although addiction can be awful and at times even life-threatening, change is possible, and there are several clear paths to achieve an addiction-free life.

Parents can also feel hope because they can turn for help from our Creator who promised he would deliver us from darkness and back into the light. David came to this knowledge out of a desperate need. He writes, "Fear and trembling have beset me; horror has overwhelmed me"(Psalm 55:5 NIV). Many times, David wanted to run away from his circumstances to give up the battle. "Oh, that I had wings of a dove! I would fly away and be at rest"(Psalm 55:6, 7 NIV).

Be joyful in hope, patient in affliction, faithful in prayer. (Romans 12:12, NIV)

When do you plan to reach out for help?

When I first reached out for help, I attended an Al-Anon meeting specific for parents. A few days prior, I had just broken down, falling to my knees, asking God for help. I felt desperate for God's intervention for my child's addiction. I prayed, stating, "I am willing to give my life and will over to you, God. I will surrender. I will do anything you ask if you will help me in my hour of need." This prayer was something that I had always been afraid to say, let alone commit to. Despair and pain can bring us to our knees, especially when it comes to our children.

My stepdaughter had been attending AA for many years and had access to a good network of people and resources in the addiction field. When I told her about my daughter's addiction problems and that I needed help for myself, she recommended I attend an Al-Anon meeting that was specific for parents with an addicted child. The meeting was a half-hour driving time away; and feeling much shame and guilt, the tug of procrastination set in. Thank goodness, I had the sense and humility to take what I thought at the time was a big bold step and attend my first meeting.

That first meeting was tough, but right away I knew I belonged. I cried a lot while I listened to parents describing and sharing their personal experiences. It brought back hope into my life as I listened and learned from the topics of discussion. I realized the importance in having group support along with individual support from a pastor or professional addiction counselor. We all need help at some point in our life and this was certainly a time for me.

> I say to God my rock, why have you forgotten me? Why must I go about mourning, oppressed by the enemy? My bones suffer mortal agony as my foes taunt me, saying to me all day long, where is your God? (Psalms 42:9–10 NIV)

Where is God in our hour of crisis?

If there is a God, where is He when we need Him most? Where is He in our pain and despair? Good question! In Romans 8:28 (NIV), Paul says, "And we know that in all things God works for the good of those who love him, who have been called according to his purpose." How in the world does this verse help us in our world of addiction, especially when it comes to alcohol/drug addiction in our child? Today the entire world seems to be in chaos; why doesn't God step in to prevent disastrous things from happening?

God's plan has changed from its original inception where God wanted us to live in perfect harmony with him. However, he gave us the ability to choose; and we chose to be disobedient, to go against God's perfect plan for us. In the prose book of Genesis, we are given a visual symbol of how Adam and Eve went against God's one rule, do not take the forbidden fruit from the tree of life. We are all descendants of the "one man," Adam. When Adam sinned, the sting of death fell on him. And the result in all the human race is sin, rebellion against God.

What would you do as a parent if your child clearly breaks the most important rule in your household? Would you ignore it or let him suffer the consequences of their bad choice? How else do they learn if it were not for an understanding of clear boundaries and the consequences of pain that come from making bad choices?

In the epistle to Romans, it states God is working all things toward our good. This is where faith comes in. Do you possess the faith to believe this? Does doubt creep into your thinking because you are in constant fear? Isn't fear the exact opposite of faith? As Christians, we acknowledge our faith; no one can believe (or have faith) in Christ unless Christ gives him or her the gift of faith.

> For it is by grace you have been saved, through faith—and this is not from yourselves, it is the gift of God—[9] not by works, so that no one can boast. (Ephesians 2:8–9, NIV)

Do you understand that you are not alone?

Having a child struggling with addiction can lead to many painful days filled with anguish and distress. This agonizing situation can cause you to feel hopelessness and aloneness. When the pain reaches a level that tempts the loss of sanity, you can turn to God for strength and encouragement. The strength and encouragement will likely take many forms. As a Christian parent, God will give you permission to be honest about your guilt, shame, fears, and anguish, along with the tools you need so that you don't get lost in the consequences of your child's poor choices.

One of the ways God might show you is a path that leads to finding a support group, like PAL, Al-Anon, or Celebrate Recovery. Group support can be a powerful way for you to connect with other parents who have walked in your shoes. Group support can teach you about addiction and recovery, helping you feel stronger and more capable when you face difficult situations.

Another path can be found by reaching out to experts in the field, such as an addiction counselor. An addiction counselor has a wealth of knowledge that can help you become informed, giving you a feeling of empowerment, lowering your stress, and lessening your fears. By increasing your understanding of addiction and the issues and behaviors that pursue, you will feel more capable when you are faced with a difficult situation.

Sometimes it can be easier to turn to books and the internet on addiction, setting you on a path to discover stories about other parents facing the same issues. Other books and the internet can teach you about changing your behaviors such as enabling and codependency. Don't let ignorance be your downfall. God will direct your footsteps. You should not live in fear and dread of the future. Put yourself in the care of God daily.

> Ask and it will be given to you; seek and you will find; knock and the door will be opened to you. For everyone who asks receives; the one who seeks finds; and to the one who knocks, the door will be opened. (Matthew 7:7–8, NIV)

Chapter 1

Denial
Avoiding the Truth

Denial is the worst kind of lie…because it is the lie you tell yourself. (Michelle A. Homme)

Why confront denial through the grief process?

Grief is something that is unavoidable when you learn about your son or daughter's addiction to alcohol or drugs. Like a tornado, having an addicted child can damage and destroy everything in its path. In the addiction world, we are told that one addicted person adversely affects nine others. As William Coleman puts it in his book *Parents with Broken Hearts*, "Pain will rip out whatever it can and destroy it. But smart parents will not let suffering take their spirit."[2] The nightmare of addiction in a loved one can bring parents to their knees in despair and grief, becoming lost in brokenness.

When people say they understand what you are experiencing, they really don't. They might understand the feelings but not your particular situation because everyone's loss is personal and private. Your loved one has gone astray, and it may feel like a death. Grief can be brutal, zapping the life right out from under you because grieving is a process that will take time for you to recover. The hopes and dreams that you had for your child seem like a lost cause. Recognizing the loss of those shattered dreams can be devastating and overwhelming, as well as the grief that accompanies destroyed aspirations; it can be deep and poignant. After time, the pain and grief will start to destroy other relationships, impacting your ability to trust people. This can lead to superficial relationships where you don't really care about the people. You're just trying to avoid any future relational losses.

Where are you in this grieving process? Better understanding of these eight stages of grief, you will begin to realize where you're at in the grieving process. You will also be able to realize any myths about grieving you might have and how it is affecting you.

The most important thing for you to remember is not to deny your feelings or look away from your misfortune. English poet and hymnodist William Cowper described grief itself as medicine. "Grief cleanses the anguish from our souls and sets us back up on the path of life so we can dance. Grieving is the process God uses to bring us to a place of wholeness. Grieving is His great gift to us. It is a necessary part of our journey."[3] In order for you to move beyond your grief, you will need to learn how to deal with having an addicted child. Don't isolate and detach from your feelings. Join a support group where you can feel safe sharing your feelings rather than burying them. Even though it may seem impossible, you must accept and embrace your child's addiction in order to truly work through it and recover. By embracing the situation, you will learn to move through the eight stages of grief at a faster pace, strengthening your resolve and character.

> The Lord is close to the brokenhearted
> and saves those who are crushed in spirit.
> (Psalm 34:18, NIV)

Could you be in denial, ignoring the obvious?

In the beginning of your son or daughter's addiction to drugs/alcohol, it's easy to miss the signs. It's common for a parent to miss the red flags that that can indicate your child might be abusing drugs. It's simple to ignore the obvious, especially when your child has gotten to be an expert in creating "smoke and mirrors" to hide their addiction. You may have been ignorant for a time until it smacked you straight across your face. It's easy to miss the obvious signs of drug usage because you were never trained to recognize them. Once you know for sure there is an addiction issue, you should not procrastinate but confront it head on.

It has been said that procrastination is the art of keeping up with yesterday. It's much easier to put off what you know you should do today to tomorrow. We all have done it. When confronting addiction issues in your son or daughter, it can be very difficult, as well as overwhelming. Of course, you don't want to believe what you think you see. You secretly tell yourself that you are probably making a mountain out of a molehill, and your young adult child has just been doing a little experimenting like a lot of other young adults. But the fact remains that drugs and alcohol are dangerous, especially to a child's brain that has not fully developed (age twenty-six to twenty-eight).

According to Mike Speakman, most addicts go through three main stages in their addiction:

1. The honeymoon stage, when drugs/alcohol are used for relief from physical or emotional pain or pleasure.
2. The coping stage, where the person "needs" the drugs/alcohol to function.
3. The desperation phase, where drugs/alcohol become the entire focus of living.[4]

It's important for parents to understand the signs of each of these stages. Don't ignore reality. Your silence or lack of action might be interpreted as condoning the behavior. Rather than procrastinating about the obvious, join them to discuss and work together to fight against the progression of their addiction. Procrastination can be a source of a great deal of needless anxiety.

> Whoever watches the wind will not plant;
> whoever looks at the clouds will not reap.
> (Ecclesiastes 11:4, NIV)

Is denial causing dysfunction in your family?

A functional family is one where healthy emotional, psychological, and spiritual growth is cultivated among family members. Within a troubled family, there may be a member that is an alcoholic/addict. In this troubled family, the dynamics will differ from that of a normal family. "A dysfunctional family will express itself through a codependent family system, where it will try and survive through approaches using minimizing, projection, intellectualizing and denial."[5]

Minimizing is done by acknowledging there is a problem but making light of it. *Projection* is used by blaming the problem on someone else to the point of one member becoming the scapegoat to bear the family's shame. *Intellectualizing* is used to try and explain the problem away, believing that excuses and explanations will resolve the problem. *Denial* in a family is a strategy used to convince the family that there is no problem.

The dysfunctional family system will discourage the discussion of issues and feelings. A normal family will develop healthy communication where they feel free to discuss issues and feelings. Dysfunction in a family will create an atmosphere of fear, developing a need to shut itself off from the outside world, isolating and keeping family secrets to themselves. The dysfunctional family will adapt unnatural roles, making it difficult for any member to grow in confidence and self-esteem.

Dysfunction in a family, burdened with a member that is an alcoholic/addict, will develop rules that encourage unnatural patterns of relating to each other and people outside the family unit. These rules include the following: don't express feelings openly and honestly, think of the other person first rather than be selfish, don't have fun, don't challenge the family rules, don't rock the boat, don't communicate directly but rather through another family member.

All of these signs of codependency can be averted. If you face the truth, confront your denial, and want to keep your family unit healthy, seek help from a professional therapist trained in addiction and family systems.

> Blessed are those who find wisdom, those
> who gain understanding. (Proverbs 3:13,
> NIV)

Is your denial preventing your loved one from facing the natural consequences of their poor choices?

When you interfere with the natural consequences of poor choices your son or daughter has made, you probably are helping them continue in a cycle for avoiding change, changes that would mitigate their bad choices and behavior. Always coming to the rescue can hinder your adult child from gaining the motivation to seek help, from becoming a capable and responsible adult in charge of their own life. It is easy for parents to slip into codependency behavior when you're in denial and treating your adult child as if they are still a child.

Most parents need to learn to help their adult children less. When your child abuses alcohol/drugs, they usually show a lack of gratitude along with a rebellious attitude. Having a rebellious attitude is usually a diversion for your child rather than facing the real issues that plague them. A common game your addicted son or daughter will play is for him/her to do something bad to get you to try and control them so they can get angry over your efforts to control, which in turn justifies their reasoning to abuse drugs/alcohol. This crazy cycle will continue unless something changes. The change has to begin with you by helping your child less.

As a more knowledgeable parent, you will gradually make the changes necessary to help move your child forward. By not allowing them the opportunity to manipulate you, you are compelling them to stand on their own, becoming a responsible adult. The Chinese word for *crisis* is written with two brush strokes. The first stand is for danger and the second for opportunity. In other words, by letting them suffer the consequences of bad choices, not helping them fix it, you are opening up their mind for finding the better way to live, a life void of alcohol and drugs.

> Discipline your children, and they will give you peace; they will bring you the delights you desire. (Proverbs 29:17, NIV)

Are you unable to tolerate negative feelings in your child?

If you have an addicted son or daughter, you have probably witnessed him or her making destructive choices. Observing your child in the clutches of harmful patterns of substance abuse, you have probably found yourself reaching out to help fix their problems.

> As a parent you naturally want to help, but more times than not these efforts can be

more harmful than helpful. The term for this behavior/action is called "enabling" or otherwise known as "good intentions gone wrong. In other words, your "enabling" and "denial," may be making it easier for your struggling child to continue in their self-destructive activities.[6]

Some of most common enabling examples that a parent finds themselves undertaking are covering up, bailing them out of trouble, making excuses for them, giving them one more chance, and/or giving them money for essential things that you later learn went to paying for drugs.

One of the biggest factors for your enabling behavior might be your inability to tolerate negative feelings in others—i.e., child, friend, other family member, as well as yourself. The discomfort you feel when they feel sad, hurt, or are forced to suffer consequences can cause you to be depressed which in turn will unconsciously force you into a frame of mind that perpetuates your enabling behavior.

You should stay mindful that a parent's responsibility to their addicted child is to be supportive and facilitate maturity. You can empathize but not continue to fix problems that they should be learning to fix themselves. When they make mistakes, encourage them rather than protect them from natural consequences; do not rescue them. Life is full of choices and decisions. God will determine the consequences that will open their eyes, change their attitude and behavior, and ultimately transform their heart.

> Leave them; they are blind guides. If the blind lead the blind, both will fall into a pit. (Matthew 15:14, NIV)

> I pray also that the eyes of your heart may be enlightened in order that you may know the hope to which he has called you, the riches of his glorious inheritance in the saints. (Ephesians 1:18, NIV)

From the inside out, is your soul crying out?

"A good definition of soul can be the spiritual nature or the essence of you as the person, regarded as distinct from your physical body, often thought to survive after death."[7] Your spirit can feel like it is alive and well or perhaps in limbo, not feeling much, and then, in other times, feel completely empty, devoid of feeling. The feelings of the soul can be hard to put in words, especially if it's feeling vacant. Somedays all you can do is cry out for help to a God that sees, feels, and understands your desperation.

The disease of alcoholism and drug addiction is cunning, baffling, and powerful. It knows no particular sex, age, race, economic level, or religion. It can appear anytime without warning or with warning. Yes, it can appear to be a friend, giving comfort in fear and loneliness or when a person is hurting. It will give instant gratification and only ask in return for long-term suffering. It's a disease that is not taken seriously like heart disease, diabetes, or cancer. It's a hated disease, but it doesn't come uninvited. Your child has tempted the misuse of alcohol and drugs, losing control when it is too late it already has its hold.

As a parent of an adult alcoholic/addict, you may see early signs, or you may not heed the red flags that slowly appear. Remember what you just read; addiction is cunning. When you recognize the signs but choose to ignore them, making excuses for your child's attitudes and behaviors, you may be in denial. Denial ends when your child starts suffering the consequences of bad choices and behavior, and you recognize the dangers in their addiction have just begun.

At this point, your soul begins to feel afraid and in a state of despair, causing you to call out for help, to call out for help to a God that is always omnipresent and omniscient. When the oceans rise and sore, he resides in quietness. You can be still and know that he is God. If our God is for us, then who could be against us? So when our soul cries out for help, you can be assured he will be there to guide you back to safe pastures and still waters. Pray and then be still and listen!

> Then they cried to the Lord in their trouble, and he brought them out their distress. He stilled the storm to a whisper; the waves of the sea were hushed. (Psalm 107:28–29, NIV)

Are secrets keeping you in the dark?

It has been said that you are only as sick as your secrets, meaning that secrets fuel shame and isolation, making you a victim rather than a survivor. As a parent of an addicted child, you can begin to accumulate mountains of secrets, opening the floodgates for self-pity, depression, and denial. Because you want others to see only the good and positive in your child, you begin to bury shameful behavior and actions that could shed a bad light on your child and perhaps a negative outlook on you, their parent.

Having an addicted son or daughter can be likened to a hurricane, navigating tremendous winds and the debris that it can hurl at you. Like winds from a hurricane, alcoholism/drugs can bring along additional problems that include verbal, physical, and mental abuse, illness, infidelity, prison, and even death. These problems can cause embarrassment and shame, producing a desire to keep these issues under wraps. Secrets can be debilitating when they are kept in the dark. Rather, consider turning from denial, letting secrets out into the light where they can be seen and dealt with. Secrets can keep you trapped.

Support groups, trusting friends, and addiction therapists can be the best venue to share your secrets. Finding that outlet, no matter how hopeless or ashamed you may feel, can be liberating. By attending a support group, you will find many other parents who have had the same experiences and are willing to listen and help. It's important for your recovery that you find that dependable source.

God sometimes helps by speaking through others. It's important to remember that we can face any issue or challenge in life with the help from God. Frustration and confusion are not a part of God's plan for you but rather clarity and peace which can come from recognizing when he is trying to communicate with you. He listens and hears when you pray. He is never without solutions to your most difficult struggles and situations. Your part in the communication process is to learn to recognize those holy moments, those moments when God is attempting to guide and instruct you.

> I will praise the Lord, who counsels me;
> even at night my heart instructs me. I have
> set the Lord always before me. Because He
> is at my right hand, I will not be shaken.
> (Psalm 16:7–8, NIV)

Chapter 2

Shock
Facing the Truth

No Experience is a cause of success or failure. We do not suffer from the shock of our experiences, so-called trauma—but we make out of them just what suits our purposes. (Alfred Adler)

Has your child's addiction pushed you into a state of shock?

Going through a traumatic experience such as finding out that your son or daughter has addiction issues can be overwhelming. Perhaps you were in denial, making excuses for their unusual behavior until you found needles or foils in the bathroom or their bedroom, and now you realize that the possibility of your child having an addiction problem is not your imagination but a reality. Maybe your loved one has gotten into legal problems and is facing jail time. Alcohol/drug addiction can bring countless moments where you find yourself in shock.

Psychological shock can cause the brain to experience what is called "flight, fight, or freeze mode." This acute stress response is short-term but can have lasting affects to your body and brain as it attempts to recover from what is referred to as "emotional shock."

As you may already know, certain chemicals are released in your body that can affect your immune system. These responses are useful to combat anxiety but can place stress on the body, making you feel tired, weary, and tense. Over time, you might overreact emotionally to little things that normally would not bother you. Sometimes the aftereffects can cause you to feel like you are thinking unclear, causing what we call "brain fog."

Once you have felt the emotional shock from the realization that your child has addiction issues, you need to take the first steps in finding the help you need to understand and deal with a child facing addiction challenges. Your recovery will be just as important as your child's. Don't waste time in getting the knowledge, skills, attitudes, and behaviors that will have a lasting effect on your recovery and that of your adult child. Join a support group such as PAL (parents of addicted loved ones), Al-Anon, or Celebrate Recovery. You can also search for a counselor that specializes in addiction. Books about addiction such as this one can be a good resource for getting questions answered and also identifying with the gamut of emotions you are beginning to experience. Don't procrastinate; do it now.

> Jesus, hear my cry! Help me when I feel overwhelmed. Hold me when my emotions break over me in waves like a stormy sea. Calm me and make me like a contented child leaning on your chest. Thank you for never regarding me as too needy. Lord, comfort me so that I can be a comfort to others. Amen.[8]

Could pain be a major way for God getting your attention?

Difficult situations that seem to cause shock and great pain in your life are often a way for God to make you stop your busy schedule and reevaluate your situation and life. How did your life become so unmanageable? You can blame your son or daughter for the problems that stem from their abuse of drugs/alcohol, or you can take a step back and ask yourself what your role may be in this difficult situation which is causing you pain and grief. What can you do to change this almost unbearable situation you find yourself participating in?

No matter how painful the situation may be, you can find qualities and characteristics in yourself that you may have not previously recognized. Strength, courage, and faith are gifts from God that he can reinforce in you. In the midst of your busy life, you may have neglected to cultivate those God-given gifts. Your own growth, spiritually and personally, can get ignored while dealing with the day-to-day duties and obligations of life, including searching for ways to love and support your addicted child.

If you try to look at life with a "half glass full" perspective rather than a "half empty" outlook, you can learn from all of life's experiences, including the problematic and trying events. It may take patience and a willingness to progress at God's pace and not your own. Remembering the old adage, "That this too shall pass," can make it easier to understand that life can only be lived under God's time and terms and not your own. He is your Creator, wanting to guide and direct your life, if you are willing to slow down, take a deep breath, and let Him. It has been said that "pain is inevitable, but suffering is optional." You have choices just as your addicted son or daughter.

> Jeramiah pleads for restoration, "You, oh Lord, reign forever... Why do you always forget us? Why do you forsake us so long? Restore us to yourself, Oh Lord, that we may return; renew our days of old. (Lamentations 5:19–21, NIV)

Are you feeling overwhelmed?

As a parent of a son or daughter with chemical dependency, you can feel beaten down, constantly exhausted from the negative emotions that can barrage your life and question your sanity, making you feel overwhelmed and in a constant state of shock and despair.

In the book of Jeremiah, the "weeping prophet," he describes what we often experience. He is broken and agonizing over the destruction of Jerusalem. He is weeping over the spiritual condition of Israel.

Does this sound familiar? We feel broken, agonizing over the condition and addiction of our son or daughter. We feel we have been imprisoned by an enemy we don't fully understand. Our spirit has been attacked with fear, dread, and horror for our child's well-being. And like Jeremiah, we become completely dependent upon the Lord's grace and mercy for deliverance, both physically and emotionally, giving us hope and relief from our emotional pain. Through faith, we learn how to survive the agonies of our soul, recounting what we know to be true, that God is a sovereign God.

Jeremiah had a strong grasp on the sovereignty of God. And like Jeremiah, we know that God is in charge; and by staying steadfast in this knowledge, He will lead us out of our darkness and into the light again, giving us the peace and serenity that we so deeply desire. Our daily hope is most clearly ignited by counting on the Lord's love, care, and compassion for us. These truths are the basis for walking in faith.

> O Lord, thou has pleaded the causes of
> my soul. (Lamentations 3:58, NIV)

Are you questioning your sanity?

Albert Einstein described *insanity* as "doing something the same way over and over again and expecting different results." After a period of time, parents of an addicted child grow weary, wondering if they are going to lose their mind over the shock and fear that a child can cause with their substance-abuse problems and issues. They may feel that they are at their wit's end, knowing that their child is showing signs of more and more dependence on their drug of choice. The obvious signs can send shock waves down your spine.

Have you heard the saying, "The present moment is all we have?" *Mindfulness*, or being mindful, is being aware of your present moment. Of course, we all have plans, goals, and a vision for tomorrow, but learning to stay in the moment has many benefits for you when you are sometimes questioning your sanity and its relation to your child's addiction issues. Mindfulness is saying you are here or there with no other purpose than being awake and aware of that moment. Jon Karat-Zinn said, "Wherever you go, there you are." One of the ways to stay in the moment is to be silent, listen to the sounds around you, smell the fragrance in the air, or let your eyes behold the beauty of your surroundings. Be aware of each breath you take as it comes and goes.

When you learn to practice mindfulness, it can bring many benefits to your emotional and physical health along with your relationships. Using this amazing tool for stress management and your overall wellness can be used at any time and any place, bringing lasting results. A good mindful exercise is meditation used throughout the ages as a simple technique to quiet the mind. Practicing this technique can reverse your stress response, protecting you from dealing with chronic stress. While practicing meditation, your heart rate slows down along with your breathing, causing our blood pressure to normalize. To start using this technique, it would be useful to find a quiet place. Meditation can begin with just five minutes and grow to a twenty-minute session. The more you learn to use this technique, the easier it becomes to maintain the meditation exercise.

When new information hits you and puts you in a state of shock, focusing on the sound and rhythm of your breathing will have a calming effect and help you stay grounded in the present moment. First you must sit, lie, or stand in a relaxed position while slowly inhaling through your nose, counting to five in your head. After inhaling, let the air out from your mouth slowly, counting to eight in your head as it leaves your lungs. Repeat five times. I practice this as I lie in bed, trying to quiet by body sufficiently enough to fall asleep. As you have probably experienced, sleep is usually difficult for parents with an addicted son or daughter.

> Instead, it should be that of your inner self, the unfading beauty of a gentle and quiet spirit, which is of great worth in God's sight. (1 Peter 3:4)

Are you married and in shock because of your addicted son/daughter?

Whether you are married or single, both situations can be a blessing and a curse. If you're married, you should have the support of one another which can be a huge blessing while dealing with the shock of your child's addiction and struggling with the issues that present themselves. On the other hand, if you are not on the same page with regard to setting boundaries, it can be a setback for your child gaining sobriety. Your addicted child will more than likely use this break in your marriage bond to their own selfish benefit, manipulating and setting one parent against the other.

We learn through organizations like PAL (parents of addicted loved ones) that parents must focus on their marriage first and, at all costs, stay on the same page in order to have a united position, working as partners and as a team. The addiction of your child would divide your family without agreement and unity in place. As husband and wife, you need to have a separate life, as well as a family life. You need to plan fun activities together or with friends and perhaps a trip for just the two of you.

Another principle to remember is that it is very important to move forward together, educating yourselves on addiction while incorporating ways to enhance your child's progress toward sobriety. There is a program with a curriculum to help your child recover from addiction, and you need to learn it. Your child is on an emotional and spiritual journey, and his/her journey should be reason to encourage you to focus on your own journey of spiritual and emotional growth. Many parents that have chosen to follow the PAL program will later relate how it took them from despair to hope, from ignorance to knowledge and helped them stay the course that gave them their child back, as well as their own lives.

> Again I tell you that if two of you on earth shall agree about anything you ask for, it will be done for you by my Father in heaven. For where two or three come together in my name, there am I with them. (Matthew 18:19–20, NIV)

Are you a single parent in shock?

Whether you are single or married, you will find that dealing with an addicted adult child is very challenging, if not perplexing. As a single parent, you will need to make decisions on how you respond to your son or daughter's attitude and behavior on your own, without needing to check with a spouse. Dealing with the initial shock of the situation and making decisions on your own without the support of a spouse can be extremely difficult. However, because so many parents find it difficult to align on the decision-making process when dealing with an addicted child, it might be easier for you as a single parent to make them on your own. Whatever the case, it is a good policy for yourself to have the support of a good therapist or support group.

For example, when dealing with the initial shock of your addicted child's addiction, it can be easy to say yes to every monetary request they make. Maybe you've bailed out your son or daughter from jail once, thinking they have probably learned their lesson only to find out that they go right back to abusing substance the next day. Since you do not have a spouse to help you make those decisions, you will need to turn to someone else for support and counsel. It's not wise to try and do this on your own because you will spend a lot of time second-guessing your decisions.

Instead, reach out and lean and learn from those who have had similar experiences.

Your primary goal whether a single parent or married should be to refuse to take responsibility for your adult son or daughter's actions or inactions. As you continue on this journey, you will probably learn that by doing less, you're actually doing more, accomplishing new habits and goals sooner than later. Because their addiction has caused them to act and behave like a child, parents can easily forget that they are adults. You will soon find out that doing less goes against a parent's natural instincts, so you will have to do quite a lot of work and practice in learning new behaviors. Just remember it might not feel right until your under-standing and knowledge of the disease starts to sink in. Don't give up, God won't. He is in charge and is there for you and your child with hope, courage, and strength.

> The Lord himself goes before you and will be with you; he will never leave you or forsake you. Do not be afraid; do not be discouraged. (Deuteronomy 31:8, NIV)

Are you a grandparent in shock?

If you are a parent of a child that is addicted to alcohol/drugs, your life has been turned upside down with fear, guilt, shame, and distress beyond what you or anyone can imagine. When you add grandchildren into the scenario, everything that could go wrong more than doubles, and the devastation a grandparent feels can be shocking and overwhelming. The lessons you can learn from support meetings becomes twice as hard to carry out because now it entails innocent children that had no choice to be born to an alcoholic/addict. So how do you love and support your grandchildren? In this situation, it will be more difficult for you to let your addicted son or daughter suffer the consequences of bad choices that come from distorted thinking caused by alcohol/drugs.

It doesn't matter how old the grandchildren are, all age children should be nurtured and loved by their parents. Here are some of the hard facts grandparents find themselves dealing with:

According to studies of families with substance use disorders (SUDs),

> The studies reveal patterns that significantly influence child development and the likelihood that a child will struggle with emotional, behavioral, or substance use problems... Families in which there is a parental SUD are characterized by an environment of secrecy, loss, conflict,

violence or abuse, emotional chaos, role reversal, and fear.[9]

If your grandchild is being neglected by your son or daughter, you need to call the Child Protective Services. They will come out and investigate the situation. If the circumstances are so bad that the child needs to be taken from their parent/parents, they will find a temporary home for them until it becomes safe for the child/grandchild to return. CPS will contact the closest of kin (which well might be you) to see if they are able and willing to take care of the child until the situation becomes safe for them to return back home. It's important to remember that you can't just take the grandchild. You will need the help of CPS unless you are willing to hire an attorney and go to court. Sometimes this action will shock your child into seeking help rather than losing their child, coming to grips with the reality of the severity of their addiction. Helping them find their bottom can be a good thing.

> Even to your old age and gray hairs I am he, I am he who will sustain you. I have made you and I will carry you; I will sustain you and I will rescue. (Isaiah 46:4, NIV)

Have you confronted your addicted son or daughter?

Now that you are past the stage of denial and getting through the shock of your new reality, are you ready to confront your addicted child? When you confront is as important as how you confront. In other words, direct confrontation can be dangerous, especially if your son or daughter is under the influence of drugs or alcohol at the time. Usually confrontations while under the influence will end up in screaming matches, putting you on the defensive. It's all too common for the child to throw unfair accusations at you that they won't remember the next day with you walking away feeling bruised and broken for days. Rather, the rule of thumb, so to speak, is to wait until your adult child is not under the influence.

One method for confronting your loved one is the direct method asserting a straightforward but compassionate approach. Using this method, you convey your belief to your adult child that they have addiction issues, urging them to commit to a meaningful recovery program. Sometimes, this is referred to as an intervention. The reason you would want to confront your addicted son or daughter is to help them, doing what you can to help them break their denials. Communication skills are important when trying to achieve a direct method of confrontation, planting seeds, so to speak. Planting seeds that can help break denial is a series of sincere messages communicated in a mutually respectful manner by family members and close friends in a group setting.

However, another affective confrontation approach is the indirect style. This method uses an indirect approach, asking related questions such as, "What do you think about the idea that addiction is a family problem, not an individual one, John?" Using this approach, you are not making judgmental or sarcastic remarks that demand change. This style of confrontation using these kind of statements over weeks or months can have a real emotional impact on your addicted child. This method of "planting seeds" would also help prepare your addicted child for a direct confrontation if they should stay in denial. Sometimes it is impossible to tolerate the effects of your child's behavior, so an indirect method would not work for you.

If you can tolerate your adult child's behavior and they are not close to hitting their bottom, you can take the patient approach, making respectful comments and statements about inner pain, self-medication, addiction, and recovery. Aim to help your adult child hit a true bottom rather than trying to control their addiction.

> Love is patient, love is kind. It does not
> envy, it does not boast, it is not proud. It
> is not rude, it is not self-seeking, it is not

easily angered, and it keeps no record of wrongs. Love does not delight in evil but rejoices with the truth. It always protects, always trusts, always hopes, and always perseveres. (1 Corinthians 5, NIV)

Can you get over the shock in order to move forward with an intervention?

Considering a formal intervention and seeking a professional to help with this task means you are moving past the stage of denial and shock, wanting to deal with facts at hand. Consider first asking your child if they think they have an addiction to alcohol or drugs. When they open up and answer this question, it's important to listen closely without interruption. As a parent, you need to accept your loved one's reality. If you don't agree, it won't do any good to argue because it gets you nowhere. By listening to your son or daughter, you can begin to understand their perspective, giving you an idea with what you are dealing with. Their perspective is important because you are then able to better lead them to the truth. Their truth is important to understand because you can only lead them from their reality, not what you think it actually is.

Your son or daughter might be in denial. When asked, they may say, "No, I don't think I am addict." At this point, ask, "Have drugs or alcohol been a problem for you in the past?" If they answer yes, then ask, "What do think you need to do for your alcohol or drug problem?"[10] The answer they give is where the plan should begin to move forward for helping them treat their addiction. So would it be better to seek a professional interventionist, a cooperative approach, or allow them to continue suffering the consequences of their addiction (hit their bottom) until they are ready to get professional help. Maybe your child would be willing to get a professional assessment at a treatment center or from an addiction therapist. Whether your child thinks they have an addiction problem or not, it's important not to enter into arguments on the subject but rather enter into discussions on help that is available either way.

As a parent, you want to be careful of labeling your child as an addict. Being labeled an addict may be difficult for them to face. You can help lead them to realizing they may be an addict without calling them an addict. Seeking help for addiction is not all about abstinence from drugs or alcohol. When speaking to your child, you can also point out that treatment or counseling can help them with life skills, as well as adult coping skills, helping them realize the benefits of this knowledge.

> Commit to the Lord whatever you do, and your plans will succeed. (Proverbs 16:3, NIV)

Are you ready for the journey?

Now that you are getting over the shock of learning that your child has become dependent on alcohol/drugs, you need to set out on a new journey of hope. Clinging to hope will be difficult on this journey but very achievable. Parenting an addicted adult child requires a different set of parenting skills than parenting a normal child. This journey is going to require you to change. If you have the desire and courage to make the changes necessary, you will achieve joy, serenity, and peace again. No longer will you waste time blaming yourself, others, and God for your situation but rather taking the steps necessary for new knowledge and practice of new learning. At different points on this journey, you will begin to see your adult child reacting in a more positive, healthy way. At this point, you will know it is because of the changes you have made. Even though things are not yet where you want them to be; but the small changes, you do realize, taking place with your loved one gives you a glimmer of change reinforcing your hope.

According to Mike Speakman, there are eleven principles of family education that can provide you a framework for your journey:

1. There is a curriculum to your loved one's recovery from addition; you can learn it.
2. Your loved one's recovery is not an event. It's a process through time, a journey.
3. Your loved one's journey is one of emotional and spiritual growth.
4. This journey is a marathon, not a sprint.
5. Your loved one's journey of growth invites you to focus on your journey of growth.
6. Despite appearances, you have no control over your loved one's journey, only your own.
7. Your loved one's journey is not your journey.
8. Your journey forces you to face and confront some unpleasant realities of life.
9. You are not alone on your journey, and all the help you will need is available.
10. The further you go on your journey, the more it helps your loved-one.
11. You can get to a point on your journey where, no matter what your loved one does, you will either

know what to do, or know where to find out what to do."[11]

"2 through whom we have gained access by faith into this grace in which we now stand. And we rejoice in the hope of the glory of God. 3 Not only so, but we also rejoice in our sufferings, because we know that suffering produces perseverance; 4 perseverance, character; and character, hope." (Romans 5:2–4, NIV)

Chapter 3

Release of Emotions
Frustration with the Truth

Unless we have that moment of chaos, followed by emotional release of realization, nothing will be remembered. (Chuck Palahniuk)

Has fear creeped into your life?

As a parent of a child who has an alcohol or drug addiction, you may often be blinded by fear, the fear for your beloved child who has made some bad choices and now is suffering from the consequences of those bad choices. Fear tests our faith!

Do you remember reading about Jesus when he had spent all day speaking to the multitudes? When evening came, he commanded his disciples to sail with him to the other side of the lake. As they sailed across the sea, Jesus lay down and fell asleep. But a squall came down on the lake, threatening to submerge the boat. The disciples panicked, so they woke up the Lord.

Addiction is your "squall" sweeping down on your child's life, as well as your own. A sense of fear or confusion, even panic, tends to overtake you when your "boat starts rocking." You, like the disciples, often get "scared to death." Suddenly your life is out of control, and your circumstances feel hopeless; you begin to feel desperate and alone.

The Lord's first words upon awakening are amazing. He got up and rebuked the wind and the raging waters; the storm subsided, and all was calm. He then turned to the disciples, asking, "Where is your trust, your confidence in me?"

The Lord is asking very direct questions. He is asking you the same questions in the midst of your "squalls." "Why would you not place your faith in me? Why are you not confident that I, as your shepherd and your friend, will deliver you safely to the other side?"

The enemy can create major disturbances in your life. By yourself, you have no ability to protect yourself from these satanic attacks. Your hope is that the Holy Spirit will bless you with an understanding in such a way that you will, by faith, place your trust fully in the Lord and Savior, who loves you unconditionally, rebuking any fear that comes at you from the enemy.

> Be self-controlled and alert. Your enemy the devil prowls around like a roaring lion looking for someone to devour. Resist him, standing firm in the faith. (1 Peter 5:8, NIV)

Are you feeling completely defeated?

When your child's problems and issues from addiction loom over you, do you feel completely defeated, barely able to put one foot in front of the other? It's not uncommon for a parent to feel the weight of defeat after traveling on this journey for much longer than expected. Sometimes, it can feel like a never-ending treadmill, unable to stop the progression of the insane behavior seen in your adult child. Barely holding on by a thread, you begin to believe that you will not likely be capable of overshadowing this destructive power and watching your unfortunate circumstance come to an end. Thriving again seems an impossibility.

These frustrating experiences that you and other parents have had to undergo can be life-altering and traumatizing. The joy and zest for life can extinguish itself. Your child has pushed you to your breaking point. The pain caused from this heart-wrenching experience has brought you to your knees, deflating your spiritual, emotional, and mental ability to cope with life, maybe even to the point of losing your will to live.

This is when resilience is needed to push back on your defeated attitude. Instead of collapsing under the heavy pressure of feeling doomed to a life of fear and hopelessness, you can help your dreadful situation by making some changes, but the changes must start with you. In AA, it is commonly said, "If nothing changes, nothing changes." That's exactly right! You can't control or cure your addicted child. They must want recovery for themselves. The only thing you can control in the relationship is you. Simply explained as a math formula: $1 + 2 = 3$. If the numbers 1 or 2 represent you and your child and one of the numbers change, the outcome changes. You, like other parents that have a son or daughter with addiction issues, need to realize that when you are dealing with an addicted adult child, parenting methodology has to change. This change process for you will be slow, coming incrementally. With the right guidance and changes you are willing to make, you soon will begin to see positive behavioral changes in your child. Reach out to a support group like PAL and learn the lessons.

> So do not fear, for I am with you; do not be dismayed, for I am your God. I will strengthen you and help you; I will uphold you with my righteous right hand. (Isaiah 41:10, NIV)

Are you overwhelmed with grief?

The Bible describes grief as deep mental anguish, full of sorrow. As a parent of an addicted child, I know how gut-wrenching grief can be. Parents love their children unconditionally. From the minute they are born, we begin to dream of a life for our child full of success and promise. We pour out heart and soul into helping them grow into kind, caring, and God-loving young adults.

Somewhere along the journey, you may notice small violations of the values you tried to impress on them. The environment, the friendships, and the culture all have impact on your child. You cannot completely protect them from the world they live in. Maybe you have tried by not letting them go to private or public schools, homeschooling them until their high school years. But then what? Have they been so protected that they have not gained life's coping skills to do deal with hard choices that they need to make on their own? Maybe they grew up resenting the protection you have tried to cultivate in their lives. They may rebel or turn to other methods of coping with life's difficulties such as alcohol and drugs. Drugs are prevalent in our society, and no one can deny the impact that it can have on your child's life when they begin to cope by self-medicating.

A chemically addicted child can enter into periods of crisis again and again, their issues never getting resolved. When they continue in their addiction without seeking help, the negative effects of their addiction on a parent, as well as other members of the family, can bring the worst grief a parent could possibly experience. These waves of pain and misery can start to destroy any hope for life to return to normalcy. I cannot imagine experiencing greater depths of discouragement and hopelessness. If it were not for Al-Anon, PAL-group, and my strong faith, I could not have kept my sanity.

> For men are not cast off by the Lord
> forever. Though he brings grief, he will

show compassion, so great is His unfailing love. For he does not willingly bring affliction or grief to the children of men. (Lamentations 3:31–33)

Have you placed the care of your child in God's hands?

As a parent of an addicted son or daughter, you may have been mentally struck with the possibility of losing him/her to an overdose. It is not unusual for parents to become obsessed with their child's addiction problems, causing worry and fear. Addiction is a serious disease that can become a life and death reality. National news reminds us daily of the serious epidemic that is gripping our nation, our young men and women, as well as older adults. The statistics are overwhelming. How do you come to terms with this frightening scenario?

As a Christian, you are given the gift of the Holy Spirit that brings about faith and trust in God, our creator. The stories in the Bible reflect the strength and courage that were given to such mortal men as Abraham and Job. Under devastating circumstances, they kept their faith and turned everything over to God, trusting in his promises for eternal life. Abraham was tested in his faith with the command to sacrifice his dearly beloved son, Isaac, on Mount Mariah. Job's faith was tested when he lost everything, including his home, children, and riches. Do their stories ring true in your life? Are you able to cling to the hope that your Creator knows what's best for you and your loved one? Picture the fortitude and faith it took for Abraham to lay down his beloved son on that altar. Now picture yourself doing the same thing with your child. This is the ultimate meaning of the AA slogan, "Let go and let God."

Abraham and Job's entire hope was based on their certainty of a future life with purpose and meaning in which they would participate with the Lord in a resurrected body. Is that your certainty today, your daily mind-set in the face of your current circumstances? Is your faith solidly based on Biblical realities that far exceed human reasoning? The key is to know these truths and experience the kind of solid conviction we see demonstrated in Abraham's and Job's life. A reminder to us all is found in this verse:

> Faith comes by hearing and hearing by the
> Word of God. (Romans 10:17, NIV)

Why are expectations referred to as "future resentments?"

In *The Big Book* (*Alcoholics Anonymous*), the addict is reminded that expectations are referred to as "future resentments." Resentments tend to originate from failed hopes or expectations for another person.

Expectations can also be false hopes or beliefs that a parent of a chemically dependent child tends to grasp onto when they see improvement in their child's attitude or behavior. This enthusiasm can be generated from the fact that your son or daughter is doing well in a recovery program or starting to take responsibility for their poor decision-making. Whatever the reason, be very careful to be "realistic" in order to avoid the disappointment that is almost certain to come when your child relapses.

It is normal for a parent to get their hopes up when they see their addicted child making strides in maintaining their sobriety. Expectations are a normal part of life of being human. It only becomes problematic when you let your expectations reach a level that is unrealistic for your addicted son or daughter to achieve. Progress is said to be two steps forward and one step back. Addiction is a very difficult disease to control. In the process of recovery, there will be many bumps in the road. Rather than setting your expectations too high, it would be wise to be "cautiously optimistic," downplaying the chances for success so that you don't suffer the harsh pain that might come when those expectations are not met.

Another good reason for you to maintain more realistic expectations is to prevent resentment that could ensue when your child has a relapse or setback. Often, in your mind, you will have an unrealistic expectation for your chemically dependent child; and when they have a setback, you unknowingly form a resentment toward them for not living up to your expectation for success. When you are let down by a setback in their recovery, you develop fears that trigger anger and disappointment, allowing resentment to unknowingly take place. It's your responsibility to manage your expectations, their prospects for success.

> The LORD makes firm the steps of the one who delights in him; though he may stumble, he will not fall, for the LORD upholds him with his hand. (Psalm 37:23–24, NIV)

Are you losing your patience?

Most of us would agree on how little patience we really have when it comes to dealing with an addicted child. As you may already realize, we live in a society that demands instant gratification. We want instant coffee, instant food, instant money from the bank machine, and instant answers to our questions and dilemmas. When it comes to your son or daughter's addiction, are you looking for the instant answer to all the problems created by his/her addiction? After coming to an Al-anon or a PAL meeting, you soon realize that recovery is a process that will take time. Change takes time with no immediate solutions. In a PAL meeting, we are reminded that recovery is "not a sprint, it's a marathon." Everyone has dark times in their life even if there are no addiction issues. It's in the process for a more peaceful and joyful life that will most likely make us happier and stronger. Instant relief is not just around the corner, but our faith tells us we are exactly where God wants us to be.

One of our challenges as believers is how to gain enough patience in the midst of our trials, tribulations, and temptations. Christ Himself is the source of patience. He alone grants us the patience to endure. Our desire for patience, our need to be patient, drives us to a higher faith in our Savior.

Using the Al-Anon slogan, "One day at a time," you can learn that your recovery is a process, realizing that no matter what is happening with your addicted child, you will be able to keep moving forward in regaining your own life back that has been lost in the drama from your loved one's addiction. Every step you take on the path of recovery will move you closer to a more healthy self, as well as a more serene life.

The apostle Paul explains that we experience God's love in our hearts as a result of Him supplying us with His love in the midst of our trials and tribulations.

> We also rejoice in our sufferings, because
> we know that suffering produces persever-

ance; perseverance character, and character hope. (Romans 5:4, NIV)

Do you feel overcome with worry?

As a parent of an addicted son or daughter, you are most likely feeling challenged. At times, you may feel overcome with worry. There are many things to worry about when dealing with addiction issues, especially your child's safety. However, when you become consumed with worry, it is the time to stop and take a deep breath and make a plan for a healthier way to live.

Worry is usually caused by overthinking an issue or problem about what may or could happen. Fear and worry is about the unknown, an over exaggeration in your mind. Most things you worry about never come about. Your mind has a way of imagining the worst, what it would be like if the fear came true. It's an invisible ghost that can scare the living daylights out of anyone who yields to it.

First, if you are experiencing anxiety, take a closer look at what is causing you the most worry. Worry is not necessarily an indication that you are weak or fragile but rather an indication that some action on your part is warranted. When you try and manage your fears, it will take strength and courage because it is the constant worrying that grips and cripples you with that unstable feeling in the pit of your stomach. When you analyze your worst fears, you will most likely be able to put things in perspective.

The best way to conquer fear and let go of worry is to start moving through it one small step at a time. Face what you are worried about head on. Be afraid and do it anyway. Stop letting your mind wander into the unknown and leaning toward the worst of whatever that unknown could be. Instead, get back into the moment to calm your nerves and start thinking positive outcomes rather than the negative. Getting back into the moment is a conscious effort to change your thinking, to quiet your mind. Use your senses to help you: smell, listen, taste, touch, and observe. "All your knowledge begins with the senses, proceeds to understanding, and ends with reason," a famous quote from Immanuel Kant.

> Therefore do not worry about tomorrow, for tomorrow will worry about itself. Each day has enough trouble of its own. (Matthew 6:34, NIV)

Do you get anxious about upcoming family celebrations?

When a holiday, birthday, or other celebrations approach, it is very common for parents with an addicted son or daughter to start feeling anxious. Stress is usually caused by things you cannot change or control, so it is important to remember acceptance of those things in which you cannot change or control. Breathing deeply and repeating the Serenity Prayer throughout the day will go a long way (Grant me the serenity to accept the things I cannot change, the courage to change the things I can, and the wisdom to know the difference). Here are some key points for parents to remember:

Traditional holidays, as well as secular national holidays, should give us cause to pause and focus on what we are grateful for. Sometimes because your focus is on your addicted child and the fears that creep into your mind, you can forget to make time to pause and give thanks to our Creator for the love and joy of family, friends, the miracle of life, God's creation, and the privilege of living. In our own recovery, we can receive the gift of grace by friends, family, support groups, church, and community. When we can forgive our child's weakness, mistakes, and failures, we are showing our own ability to give grace. Our child's recovery is a process, a slow process that we cannot control. The only person we can control, and change is ourselves. Be kind, supportive, and loving during the holiday season. Try to be a model of grace.

Remember that your child is responsible for his/her own attitudes and behaviors. If he/she is having a difficult time celebrating with family and friends, allow them to make their own decision on whether to show up and if they choose to show up, when to leave. Your child is responsible for knowing his/her triggers, taking care to heed them. Don't let it disturb you if he/she suddenly bolts from the table or excuses them self. Your adult child will know when they need to disengage. Recovery is a process for them too, and they should not push themselves too quickly to try and please others rather than taking care of themselves. Allow them to walk away and center themselves.

Remember, no family is perfect. You can find humor in stressful family times by finding uniqueness, quirkiness, weirdness, as well as commonness in your family members rather than judging them and allowing drama and resentments to unfold.

Seek peace and pursue it. (Proverbs 34:14, NIV)

Chapter 4

Guilt/Bargaining
Bartering with the Truth

My mind is filled with "what if's" Easier
than facing my pain. (loveliveson.com)

Who controls your life?

As a parent of addicted child, you can often feel strongly that your life has been taken away from you. Once the knowledge that your child has been hijacked by alcohol/drugs, your outlook on life can change dramatically.

If you're like me, you love your children unconditionally, that love goes above and beyond anything you could have imagined before having children. Part of that love manifested itself in dreams—big dreams, dreams for their life as a child, an adolescent, and then into adulthood. You understand your child like no one else does; you see their strengths, understand their struggles, and think you know what's best for them. I say think because most of us have sometimes neglected preparing them for adulthood. You do too much for them. You cover up for their mistakes rather than letting them suffer the consequences of their mistakes. Watching them suffer the consequences of their mistakes is too painful, so you step in and try to fix their problems created by addiction. Problems are usually caused by making bad choices, sometimes taking an easy way out or shortcutting a process that is meant to strengthen and teach. Instant gratification is taking over the old way of earning rewards, gifts, and prizes.

The fact is that nobody controls their own life or anybody else's, even your child. Did you determine when you were born? Your parents? The color of your skin, hair, and eyes? Did you determine your gifts, abilities, and intelligence? The country in which you were born? The circumstances that flow through your life, such as contracting cancer, as well as having no say on when you will die. So I ask you, what do you have control over? The answer is only your own attitude and behavior. Even when you make decisions, you cannot predict all the events that are set in motion because of that decision.

As a Christians, in theory, you submit your life to Christ. You decide to let Him control your life. That can be scary, so perhaps you cling to the prospect of idolatry because you do not want to lose control of your life and that of your child's. The reason for idolatry (placing your child first above God) is to create a god that we can manipulate, bargain, and therefore control. The drive for autonomy or self-control is critical to the person that does not believe in God. Even as a believer, it is difficult to completely avoid. When life comes to a close, we will remember our Lord's words, "As surely as I live, says the Lord, every knee will bow before me and every tongue will confess to God" (Romans 14:11, NIV).

An important slogan in AA and Al-Anon is "let go and let God." You are much better off yielding to God's authority in this life than trying to control your destiny and that of your children.

Do you understand and agree with the three C's?

Al-Anon often refers to the three C's: "You did not cause the addiction. You can't control it, and you can't cure it." This is an important Al-anon phrase to understand and remember.

As a parent of a chemically addicted son or daughter, it is essential to understand that you did not cause the addiction. Active substance abuse involves people who actively drink or use drugs. They don't drink or take drugs because of you or me but because they are addicted. This is a fact that you must come to terms with. You can needlessly feel guilty, lecture your loved one, beg them, reason with them, threaten them, or bargain with them. Following this thought pattern, you will only prolong your struggles and eventually lose.

As a parent, you cannot control your adult child, but you can positively influence them by continuing to be good examples and role models. You can do this by putting your attention back on yourself, paying attention to your own needs, as well as others in your family. If your child is eighteen or older, they are free to make their own decisions, free to fail or succeed. You have control of your own recovery, not theirs.

If you didn't cause the addiction and you can't control it, then how can you possibly cure their addiction to alcohol/drugs? As a parent, it is very difficult to watch your loved one continue to drink or drug, but you cannot do anything to stop it or cure it. A person only has control of themselves, no one else.

The goal should be to admit you are powerless over alcohol and drug addiction and redirect your efforts and energy that you have spent on fighting your adult child's disease into your own recovery from the effects of their addiction. You now need to be willing to change the way you interact with your addicted child by first being responsible to your own health and well-being, keeping your focus where it belongs, on you.

> I will praise the Lord, who counsels me;
> even at night my heart instructs me. I have
> set the Lord always before me. Because he
> is at my right hand, I will not be shaken.
> Therefore my heart is glad and my tongue
> rejoices; my body also will rest secure.
> (Psalm 16:7–9)

Do you find yourself volunteering to help?

According to Mike Speakman, the number one rule to remember is "give no un-asked-for help; do not volunteer help."[12] Unknowingly, many parents volunteer to help their addicted son or daughter when they are asked directly or even indirectly. You have probably bought into a story your addicted son or daughter has sold you so that you feel sorry for them, giving them financial help when they should be able to handle it on their own. Even when your adult child does not ask for help directly, they may hint that they are having difficulties such as a hard time paying their bills, so you willingly oblige and pay their bills for them. When you realize they are in need, you naturally want to give them a helping hand, as most parents would want to do. Guilt can cause us to step in and try to fix our adult child's challenges.

Alcoholics/addicts get very good at manipulation, and their parents are the easiest to manipulate. Your addicted child has you trained to think for them. All your child needs to do is hint they are having difficulties, and you jump in to offer them help. Imagine what this looks like to them, offering them help when they haven't even so much as asked for help. It looks and feels like they are being treated as a child and not an adult. When you treat them like children, how can you expect them to think and act like adults, taking responsibility for themselves?

Consciously or unconsciously, your alcoholic/addict child knows the game of manipulation well. They started this "match of wits" in early childhood. They have always known their parents would jump in to help them, taking all responsibility away from them, as well as the chance to grow their self-esteem. When you begin to educate yourself on addiction, you will start viewing these conversations with your chemically dependent adult child differently, watching for the red flags that pop up when your son or daughter is obviously needing something from you. Recognizing this "match of wits" game, you can change your response, giving them the opportunity to figure out solutions on their own, imposing responsible adult behavior. Your new role will take some practice.

> Apply your heart to instruction and your ears to words of knowledge. (Proverbs 23:12, NIV)

Is guilt causing you to be an enabler?

The definition of *enabler* is doing something for someone else that they should be able to do for themselves. The enabler has a strong need to control their addicted child and perhaps others too.

Understand that a parent's enabling is born out love, concern, and guilt. However, as a parent, you need to help your child grow emotionally to become a responsible and independent adult. Your enabling behavior gets in the way of your child's need to grow up and learn to take responsibility for themselves.

Parents who have an addicted child need to change their role from enabler to parent, setting clear and concise boundaries. Also, other healthy attributes for a parent include good listening skills and encouraging positive behavior. For support in learning to evolve into a new role, seek out help from a PAL group (parents of addicted loved ones), Al-Anon, or an addiction therapist. There are also good books to help us understand our enabling nature. Consider the possibility that unhealthy helping may be giving your addicted son or daughter help in the short term but may be hurting them in the long-term.

In spite of your concern, you cannot control the behavior or attitudes of your addicted child. You are only responsible for your own behavior and attitudes. Rescuing by fixing your addicted child's problems only makes them more dependent, irresponsible, and resentful, tearing down their self-esteem. When you try reasoning with your child, scolding or using threatening techniques, you will find that it rarely works. When you accept excuses or promises from your addicted child, you only encourage further abuse and denial. You will need to be crystal clear about what is acceptable behavior in your home or when spending time together. Your home and its environment are yours to control.

"And we know that in all things God works for the good of those who love him, who have been called according to his purpose (Romans 8:28 NIV). How do you know that God is at work to bring good from pain, persecution, conflict, and confusion? In verses Romans 8:28–39, the Bible lays out solid reasons for hope in the believer's greatest trials. The reason for our hope resides in God's love.

Are you behaving like a helicopter parent?

A good definition for a *helicopter parent* is a parent who takes an overprotective or excessive interest in the life of their child. As a parent, you start off with good intentions, trying to stay engaged with your child and their lives but then find that you lose your perspective on what their needs really are, becoming too enmeshed in your relationship with them. You want to stay engaged in their lives to help build their self-confidence and provide guidance, as well as opportunities to grow; but once your parenting becomes controlled by fear and guilt by what might happen, you can lose the opportunity to teach them. Failure, along with challenges, can teach a child to develop skills which are needed as they grow into mature adults.

Some of the consequences of over parenting include decreased confidence and self-esteem, sending them a message that they can't do things without your help; you don't trust them to do this on their own, creating higher levels of child anxiety and depression. Another consequence is that your child may not develop the coping skills they need, making them feel less confident in dealing with life's stresses. As parents, we can't always be there to prevent bad things from happening, so we must step aside and let them learn from coping with loss, disappointment, and failure. A sense of entitlement can be another consequence of helicopter parenting. Parents who are always adjusting their child's social, academic, and sports involvement to fit the child's needs will help them become accustomed to always getting their way, feeling entitled.

You can avoid being a helicopter parent by looking for opportunities to take a step back and not jumping in to solve your child's problems, building reliant and self-confident kids to become adults by letting them struggle, be disappointed when failure happens, helping them work through it.

Encourage the young to be self-controlled. In everything set them an example by doing what is good. In your teaching show integrity, seriousness and soundness of speech that cannot be condemned. (Titus 2:7)

Are you playing the blame-and-shame game?

It is not uncommon for parents to blame themselves for their son or daughter's addiction to alcohol/drugs. As parents, you have nurtured and cherished your child since birth. Now, as they move into their adult years, you find yourself entrenched in the issues that revolve around your child's addiction. Maybe they are in college, on a career track, single or married or married with children. Whatever the circumstances, parents never stop being parents, especially when difficulties and dangers threaten their child.

You needn't blame yourself for not knowing what to do about your child's addiction. You had no way of knowing exactly what lay ahead. Before the addiction reared its ugly head, there might have been some signs that went unnoticed because you were probably not educated on the signs that presented themselves in your child. There is no way to know exactly what to expect before it happens. Now that you know your child has addiction issues/problems, the question is, what can you do? The answer is work on your own recovery.

The harm to you mentally has gone beyond description, causing you mental anguish, suffering, and grief. Because of the damage your child's addiction has inflicted to your own mental and physical well-being, you must begin to take steps to repair the damage. If you take these steps (join a support group, individual therapy, read books on addiction) for your own recovery, learning and educating yourself, you will be able find pleasure in your own life irrespective of the choices your child makes.

This can be one of the toughest journeys you will take, but realize that you are not alone. You can get through this. You might not be the same person after traveling on this journey, but you will become stronger and healthier through faith that is exercised through these difficulties and perils.

> He holds victory in store for the upright, he is a shield to those whose walk is blameless, for he guards the course of the just and protects the way of his faithful ones. (Proverbs 2:7–8)

Can you let go of guilt?

There is always a certain amount of guilt that comes with having a child that has succumbed to the tragedy of drug or alcohol addiction. You ask yourself: where did I go wrong? How could I have been a better parent? What was lacking in my parenting skills?

We can give in to nagging memories where we did something wrong and not making better choices in how we reacted or behaved. These memories can get in the way of moving forward in our own personal and spiritual growth, as well as how we can best help our addicted child. In PAL (parents of addicted loved ones) we can turn to the lessons that teach us how to move from unhealthy thinking/helping to healthy thinking/helping.[13]

Guilt is an unnecessary burden that can keep you from giving yourself fully and freely to the present. Admitting to past mistakes helps you move from the past into the present, allowing yourself to be human, where mistakes are common and can't always be avoided. As parents, your children sometimes expect perfection. This is an unrealistic expectation. But when you learn to admit to past mistakes, ask for forgiveness, you are allowing not just yourself but your children to grow in the knowledge that you are human with human shortcomings.

The Apostle John writes, "If we claim to be without sin, we deceive ourselves and the truth is not in us. If we confess our sins, He is faithful and just to forgive us our sins, and to purify us from all unrighteousness" (1 John 1:8–9, NIV). In other words, it is in telling the truth about our failures as human beings that your relationship with Christ is both revealed and confirmed. As God's children, we can have peace that God understands your human failings and will forgive you, helping you move forward in your faith and ability to deal with life's challenges.

> Search me, God, and know my heart; test
> me and know my anxious thoughts. See if
> there is any offensive way in me, and lead
> me in the way everlasting. (Psalm 139:23–
> 24, NIV)

Have you allowed your child to suffer natural consequences?

As a parents, we have all done our best to raise our kids with love and encouragement. If you have a son or daughter with an addiction problem, you are probably wondering where you went wrong. Maybe your child is a young adult, but you've noticed that they are emotionally immature. In the addiction field, we call this Delayed Emotional Growth (DEG).

DEG is a condition caused by substance abuse where we notice that our child has not grown into a responsible adult with good common sense, taking full responsibility for their decisions and choices. Some of the traits of DEG are lack of morals (lies, steals, breaks promises), immature self-centeredness (resents authority, expects instant gratification, excessively angry), never became their own person/

independent, depends on others to rescue them, believes they must have alcohol/drugs to cope with their life.

Delayed Emotional Growth can be caused by the abuse of alcohol/drugs in their developmental years (childhood through early twenties). Resistance to change can be caused by addiction and DEG. Change for your son or daughter can be painful because it involves challenging what is familiar, taking them out of their "comfort zone." Your addicted loved one has used alcohol and drugs to cope with the stresses of life, safety, comfort, and control.

When your child suffers from the consequences of poor choices (i.e., putting their finger in the fire, so to speak), he/she will learn quickly from their mistake and are not likely to do it again. As parents, you need to allow the consequences to happen so your child can learn and move forward in their emotional maturity. When you interrupt the natural process of your son or daughter feeling the pain from their poor choices, you are sending the wrong message: you cannot make good decisions for yourself. "I must take care of you because you cannot take care of yourself."[14] Consequences come from a place of love and compassion and are not confrontational or a means of punishment.

As a parent, you need to get out of the way and let life's experiences teach your child. The negative consequences of their poor decisions will steer them away from undesirable behavior. Allowing your child to experience the consequences of their actions, they are learning powerful lessons about life.

Paul states in Romans 5:3 (NIV),

> We also rejoice in our sufferings, because we know that suffering produces perseverance; perseverance, character; and character, hope. And hope does not disappoint us, because God has poured out his love into our hearts by the Holy Spirit, whom he has given us.

Do you think "letting go" is neglect?

For parents, the Al-Anon slogan "letting go" is a hard concept to embrace. For years, we have nurtured our children's growth into adulthood, often putting our child's life ahead of our own. Out of habit, it is not unusual for us to continue to nurture our actively using child in a way that it is not healthy because it would feel like neglect. Of course, as loving parents, we want to help cure their addiction with every means available to us.

"Detaching with love," is an Al-Anon concept in the addiction world that has been used for years for good reason. As parents, you must face the reality that you must get out of the way, handing over responsibility to your child for their own life. You don't stop loving and supporting them but rather recognize the importance of them developing their own independence by making decisions and solving their own problems. When they become responsible for their own choices in life, it gives them the opportunity to succeed, building on their self-esteem.

This process of "letting go" is easier said than done. Few will fully succeed with this concept, but you can take baby steps each day to achieve this goal. It takes courage to "let go" of what feels right and comfortable and move forward, changing your attitudes and behaviors that will allow your child the freedom to make their own choices even when you don't agree with them. With your entire being, you want to prevent them from making bad decisions that can alter their lives in dramatic negative ways.

As you grow in your own recovery, you will feel less like you must have your own way but will rather feel the freedom of "letting go," allowing God to have control of your son or daughter's life journey. You are still free to express your opinions and ideas but will allow your child and God to work out the details. As your addicted child lives their life, it is your job to "let go and let God," stepping out of the way, accepting the outcome.

So do not fear, for I am with you; do not be dismayed, for I am your God. I will strengthen you and help you; I will uphold you with my righteous right hand. (Isaiah 41:10, NIV)

Do you sometimes think your addicted child is beyond hope?

As parents of an addicted son or daughter, do you often wonder if hope is still possible? Maybe the circumstances have gotten so bad that you feel like giving up because you feel overwhelmed with discouragement, leaving you exhausted and drained of all emotions but hopelessness. No matter how much you try to convince your son or daughter to change, the behavior and attitudes remain the same. The disease has control of your child, sending them, as well as you, down a deep dark hole that seems unsurmountable; the light has almost diminished.

You ask yourself: how can I get relief from this painful situation? You feel like a deer in the headlights, so to speak, not knowing where to turn or what to do next. The solution seems impossible. When you are feeling so depressed about the situation, it helps to lean into the Al-Anon slogan: "You didn't cause it. You can't control it. You can't cure it—you don't need to contribute to it." Admit it. You are at a point where something has to change.

Ask yourself: are you willing to make changes in yourself? Maybe your energy needs to be focused on steps that will bring you relief because you are basing all your hope on your child being willing to change rather than changes that you can make in yourself. The challenge becomes too great or even impossible to change your son or daughter, so why not turn to ways that take the spotlight off your child and direct it back on yourself?

How have your behaviors/actions contributed to the problem or prolonged it? If you need help answering this question, remember this statement from Mike Speakman, PAL founder and counselor, "The first place change must take place is with you, the only person you truly can change. You must make a commitment to change your own beliefs, habits and actions. Until you do, the same cycle will simply repeat."[15]

You must learn to reach out for help. Turn and accept help from others—for example, a personal addiction counselor, a support group, such as PAL or Al-Anon, and your pastor—that will be able to give you suggestions, as well as support.

> In my distress, I called to the Lord; I cried
> to my God for help. From his temple he
> heard my voice; my cry came before him,
> into his ears. (Psalms 18:6)

Are you possibly codependent?

In the recovery realm, we recognize several definitions of codependency, but the one I identify with is "rationalized selfishness." Some psychotherapists think of it as a disease, "the disease to please."[16] Maybe this segment will help some of you perhaps recognize this characteristic in yourself. It's very difficult to come to terms with these expression; but eventually you will, later laughing at yourself for not recognizing these traits in yourself sooner. Mike Speakman states it like this, "Codependency is quite a complex subject, but can be seen simply as over-helping others to the detriment of yourself. It might also be defined as one adult helping another adult, but acting like a parent helping a child."[17]

In some extreme cases, it can be pathological with unresolved issues from the past that have been buried and not dealt with. Maybe you have suffered from child abandonment issues or been a child yourself of an alcoholic parent. Avoidance of these kind of issues can resurface eventually in codependent behavior. A workaholic, who uses work as an excuse to avoid facing childhood issues without facing the pain of resolving them, will overcompensate in other areas of their life such as overworking to avoid the pain that caused the workaholic behavior.

No matter what degree that codependency exists, it's very important for parents to change their role from parenting their child to being role models and examples of what adult attitudes and behaviors look like. As we learn in PAL meetings, it would be beneficial for parents to progress in their own recovery to the point that they can eventually apologize to their adult child for treating them like an underage child. Mike Speakman, founder of PAL, suggests it goes something like this: "We love you very much, and thought we were helping by treating you like a child. Now we realize that you deserve to be treated like the adult you are."[18]

> Do not let any unwholesome talk come out of your mouths, but only what is helpful for building others up according to their needs, that it may benefit those who listen. (Ephesians 4:29, NIV)

Are you are obsessing over your child's addiction?

Having a son or daughter addicted to alcohol/drugs can cause obsessive thinking. Obsessive thinking clogs your brain with negative thoughts, making it hard to function let alone enjoy your day. When you let your negative thinking always get in the way of sound reasoning, you can become a hostage to obsessive thinking, never giving room for enjoyable and satisfying thoughts.

If you find yourself going down this road, you must exercise your power of choice by refusing to allow obsessive thinking and guilt tripping to interrupt your normal thought process. Otherwise, those obsessive thoughts will gain steam, disturbing what could have been an otherwise enjoyable time. Your power of choice could include prayer, support from a friend, or picking up a book and reading a few pages. There are many things you can do when you recognize the danger in confronting a topic that will lead you down the path of obsessive thinking.

When we start down the dangerous path of obsessive thinking, our minds can easily turn to the worst scenarios. Your addicted child can easily give you many reasons to fear the worst, so is it any wonder our minds will follow our worst fears if we allow it? Freeing your mind from these fears by not allowing your mind to enter the danger zone of obsessive thinking in the first place is a difficult task to overcome. The first step is to pay attention to your thinking. When your mind starts to contemplate an area you know can bring about obsessive thinking, make a conscious effort to change the topic in your head to something positive, something that gives you hope that your child will recover from their addiction. Change negative self-talk to positive self-talk, repeating a positive affirmation over and over in your head until you believe it—for example, using the Al-Anon saying, "I didn't cause it, I can't control it, and

I can't cure it." Make a new positive affirmation every day and repeat it often throughout the day. You are where you are and what you are because of the dominating thoughts that occupy your mind. Your choice!

> Peace I leave with you; my peace I give you. I do not give to you as the world gives. Do not let your hearts be troubled and do not be afraid. (John 14:27, NIV)

Can you let your child stumble and fall?

Enabling is a topic that is prevalent in the addiction field. Many books are written on this subject. It is wise as a parent to learn as much as possible about this enabling behavior by finding a good book on this subject. *Codependency* can be defined as "a parent treating an adult son or daughter as if he or she were still a child."[19]

In this day and age, it is very common for parents to continue doing things for their adult child, especially when it comes to using purse strings to try and control their behavior. As a parent, you want to give them all the benefits of enjoying life, eliminating as many problems as you can from taking place. However, this is not healthy for your child, especially if addiction is in the picture. It doesn't take a child long to figure out how to manipulate their parents to get their needs met. "Instant gratification" comes to mind when I think about how children and young adults expect to have every need met by their parents/family members rather than learning to take responsibility for their own needs and happiness. This creates a challenge for your child when they were not given the opportunity to develop emotionally as they grew into adulthood.

In our PAL lessons, written by Mike Speakman, we learn that "Delayed Emotional Growth is a dysfunctional condition experienced by a child who has matured physically and intellectually but not psychologically, having difficulty coping with the normal stresses and responsibility of adulthood."[20] When life can become less than perfect, a child must learn coping skills. Coping skills are not taught but rather learned through trial and error. If a parent continues to solve all of their child's issues, they become dependent, not independent. This dependence can result in the child not feeling empowered because the message they are receiving from their parents is that they are not capable of solving their own challenges and issues. Your job should be to let them stumble and fall, feeling the pain from their bad choices. Pain is the best teaching tool, especially when it comes to dealing with your addicted son or daughter.

My mother had a saying when I would whine or complain about some insignificant incident. She would say, "Toughen up, buttercup." I got the message loud and clear.

"Train a child in the way he should go, and when he is old he will not turn from it" (Proverbs 22:6). The way he should go refers to the child's direction in life. The parents' role is to train or dedicate the child to the ways of godly wisdom. The goal is to raise a child who becomes a mature, responsible adult who loves God and others.

Out of guilt, are you using purse strings in an attempt to control your adult child?

One of the most common schemes, for parents who have an addicted son or daughter, is to try and use the power of purse strings to control their behavior. Your adult child has probably come to you for financial "help" with expenses that they should have been able to pay themselves. It could be that they don't have enough money to pay for their cell phone bill, rent, food, etc., or maybe a drug dealer is asserting pressure on them for drugs they have purchased. It can be hard to determine the true need for money when addiction is a factor.

Making changes in the way you help your chemically addicted child is important. You are probably familiar with the old saying, "Tied to their mother's apron strings," or heard the words "puppet strings." These old adages are used to convey a subliminal message of control. Because "strings" vary considerably, they are sometimes obvious and other times hard to identify. For a parent with an addicted child, it is important to learn to identify and then develop a plan to sever such strings.

Most strings are financial and the strongest control issue between parents and their children. Are you a parent who has constantly bailed out your adult child, causing your child to be insecure about whether they can be successful in life as an independent adult? By cutting financial strings, you are sending two messages, one direct and the other indirect. The first message is a direct message, a message that they are an adult and should be capable of supporting themselves. The second is indirect and more important for them to understand, you believing that they are adults capable of supporting themselves. Parents can inadvertently thwart their child from learning financial responsibility. By cutting the financial strings, you are giving them a chance to move forward as an adult, learning to handle adult tasks and taking accountability for their finances.

The first step for you to take in cutting financial strings is to make a list of the financial strings between you and your child. The second is to prioritize, making it easier to start the cutting strings process, in other words, divide and conquer.

> The rich rule over the poor, and the borrower is slave to the lender. (Proverbs 22:7, NIV)

Is this a journey you did not choose?

Do you find yourself looking at other families that have children that have not turned to chemicals to self-medicate themselves for anxiety, depression, or life's ups and downs? You ask yourself: how and why did this happen to my child? Perhaps you can't help it but find yourself having a self-induced pity party because life is not turning out the way you expected. Expectations are explained in AA as "future resentments." Because of the fear of failure, you start building resentments aimed at placing blame. Holding resentments can cause you to put the blame on others, viewing yourself as a victim. As long as you have feelings of victimization, you can never expect to get better.

Because of fear and guilt that your son or daughter has an addiction problem, you probably wanted to jump in, offering help with advice and/or money. Maybe you think, like a lot of other parents, if you throw enough money at the problem, it will go away. After a period of time, you soon begin to realize that no matter what you try, the alcohol abuse or drug addiction is not going away. It fact, if you are honest with yourself, the harder you try to fix the problem, the worse it seems to get.

As a frustrated parent of an addict, you eventually grasp the concept that no matter what you do to try and fix the problem, it isn't going away. By being smart and honest, perhaps you can admit to God and others that your help has actually interfered. In what could be your child's attempt at recovery, you run interference by interjecting your will into the situation. If you could just step away and let your adult child find his/her own way, their desire to recover might be just one step away. By allowing them to reach their bottom, you will be giving them the opportunity to start seeing a different future for themselves. Try to remember that it's their journey, not yours. Al-Anon says, "Let go and let God."

When you finally reach out and ask for help by attending an Al-Anon or PAL meeting, allowing yourself to share your feelings and emotions, you can start to put things in perspective and reverse the guilt along with your defeatist attitudes and start your own journey of recovery.

> Plans fail for lack of counsel, but with many advisors they succeed. (Proverbs 15:22, NIV)

How long have you let your child manipulate you?

Children can learn to manipulate their parents at a very young age. Using their charms and strengths to get their way can sometimes be harmless and other times it can be inappropriate and risky. It's difficult to identify manipulation because parents sometimes don't understand that it is a learned behavior. A learned behavior that you have unknowingly participated in will only perpetuate and escalate into their adolescent and young adult years. Problems of manipulation can turn into bigger issues when your child uses threats to manipulate, and you allow the behavior to continue without consequences or setting firm boundaries. A smart parent can learn to curb manipulation when they learn to recognize when they are being manipulated.

A good example of how a power struggle can play out is when you ask your child do something, and they resist your request. Usually repeated requests are then ignored, so then you tell them they can't do or have something that they want. Their temper begins to show. Their voice gets louder and harsher when you refuse to give them what they want. You may look at their display of frustration as normal anger and an inability to cope with stress when actually it's really a sign that your child is trying to manipulate the situation. Your child is trying to make a power play by verbally abusing you to get their way.

When your child starts to use this kind of power play, you need to be very cautious about how you respond. Remember that you must not give in. When they raise their voice, refuse to discuss it with them and walk away, letting them know that you will only discuss it further when they calm down. You are sending a message that the discussion is over until they learn to manage their anger.

Learning to control manipulation by your addicted son or daughter can get even more challenging. As a parent of an addict, you need to be aware of all the different ways that you are being mistreated, making firm boundaries so you can eliminate the manipulation, allowing for a normal respectful relationship.

> Beware of your friends, do not trust your brothers. For every brother is a deceiver, and every friend a slanderer. Friend deceives friend, and no one speaks the truth. (Jeremiah 9:4–5, NIV)

Chapter 5

Isolation/Depression
Sometimes the Truth Hurts

There's a lowliness that only exists in one's mind. The loneliest moment in someone's life is when they are watching their whole world fall apart, and all they can do is stare blankly. (F. Scott Fitzgerald)

Are you isolating?

When parents feel hopeless, they can sometimes start to isolate. Isolation is an outward and deeper symptom of unhappiness or even depression. It comes on gradually as you are entrenched in the middle of trying to solve your child's addiction issues. Isolation can begin to happen when you have been riding the addiction roller coaster too long. This darkness feels like prison, where there is no way to escape. Only a parent of an addicted child knows this kind of darkness and despair.

Maybe you have just received a phone call from your addicted child, and they sound desperate or in need of financial help. Maybe you have just had a terrible argument where the addicted child is lashing out at you, blaming you for all their problems. Or perhaps they have relapsed or possibly been admitted to the hospital for emergency care. There are so many scenarios that can happen when a child is dependent on drugs/alcohol.

Symptoms of isolation include a lack of energy, difficulty in falling asleep, difficulty in getting up in the morning, or maybe ignoring your hygiene and personal care. These are a few of the red flags that reveal that you are in need of help. That help can be therapy, one-on-one or group therapy (PAL or Al-Anon). The main thing to remember is to reach out for help.

God understands the despair and darkness that we are feeling. He understands our prison.

> I the Lord have called thee...to open the blind eyes, to bring out the prisoners from the prison, and them that sit in darkness out of the prison house. (Isaiah 42: 6–7, NIV)

God the Father is speaking to His servant, God the Son, in this passage. We learn that Christ will come to set prisoners free, to bring them out of the darkness of their prison.

Are you dealing with shame?

Often parents don't seek the help that is available to them by attending PAL, Al-Anon, or other support groups because of the shame they feel from having a child addicted to alcohol/drugs. Sometimes a person doesn't think they would fit in with other parents going through the same type of despair and depression that accompanies parents with an addicted child. They feel their experience is somehow different from other parents going through similar experiences. Some parents think that addiction only affects the needy and poor, and therefore they are unique in that they are from the middle class, upper class, or a more educated class of people. What can I possibly have in common with these parents of drug users/alcoholics?

In a PAL or Al-Anon meeting, you learn that it is safe to be yourself, sharing secrets that you have buried from others, even close relatives and friends. In these meetings, you learn you all have a common denominator, an addicted child. Through this common bond, you learn to share honestly with people you can trust. In PAL and Al-Anon meetings, parents value confidentiality and develop an understanding of the importance of being nonjudgmental. Your hearts learn to open up to commonness and the need to learn from valued lessons and shared experiences taught at a PAL or an Al-Anon meeting.

Shame is an excuse to avoid confronting your real needs. There is no room in a shame-filled mind for the fact that you did your best at the time, bound to making mistakes now and then but learning from those mistakes, allowing yourself to grow in self-awareness. Now is the time to confront those painful past mistakes, learning from those experiences, and in the process allowing you to create a better future. Parenting is no easy task. When feeling shame, a PAL or Al-Anon meeting can help you see your situation in a different light, casting out the feeling of aloneness and despair, replacing it with faith and hope for a better tomorrow for you, as well as your loved one.

In 2 Corinthians 1:3–4 (NIV), Paul tells us that God the Father is the one who comforts us in all our troubles so that we can comfort others. When others are troubled, we will be able to give them the same comfort God has given us.

Are you afraid of being judged?

Often when you learn that your child is addicted to alcohol/drugs, you don't know who or where to turn. You need someone to talk to. Someone who will listen and empathize with you. Because you think they might pass judgement, you hesitate to reach out. Will they think you have been a bad parent? Perhaps you're afraid they will pity you, and you don't want their pity but rather their support. Maybe they're too busy with their own problems and won't want to listen to your issues, having plenty of their own problems to handle.

During these times, you need to remember that there are thousands of parents, just like you, dealing with a son or daughter who has an addiction to alcohol/drugs. Addiction research points out that for every one person addicted to drugs or alcohol, there are nine others negatively impacted by this disease. You are not alone. You can discover that you can meet people just like yourself, desperate for answers, stressed to the limit and feeling lost.

Are you willing to ask for help, to put your pride aside to find answers to your questions? Here are some suggestions: group support such as Al-Anon and PAL-group, reading books on addiction, and strengthening your faith by staying in the Word. When you start trying to find some answers, God will give you answers. Perhaps not all the answers may come right away but rather slowly so that you have time to grasp the help and suggestions that our available. Please don't try to do this on your own. This is a journey that you deserve to be supported by others.

The patriarch Job lived in about 1800 BC. His life had turned into shambles, having lost everything, including his ten children. He had lost his fame, his fortune, and his family. But he did not lose his faith in the face of unthinkable trials and circumstances. Is that your conviction today, your daily mind-set in the face of your current situation?

> Faith comes from hearing the message, and the message is heard through the Word of Christ. (Romans 10:17 NIV)

Are you experiencing a condition called hopelessness?

Parents of an addicted child can expect to feel like they are on a roller coaster ride of pain, despair, and hopelessness. Part of the dilemma is that we don't understand addiction, giving us a feeling of being overwhelmed, wondering when this awful situation is going to end. These emotions are a common denominator for parents of an addicted child, giving you another good reason for reaching out to groups of parents with the same issues, PAL group or Al-Anon. It's a complex issue, and you can gain much knowledge by sharing your experiences and reviewing educational material with other parents. This knowledge can be beneficial to your understanding of addiction and the behavior and attitudes of your addicted child.

These feelings of hopelessness, pushing you into a state of depression, can affect every area of your life, and you might be asking yourself how long you're going to feel this way. First of all, your child's addiction and situation do not to have to completely control your life. You can have a say in what you choose to control your life. Feeling hopeless and depressed is a condition that comes when you sense that your addicted child might never get better. You can replace your feelings of hopelessness with hope by educating yourself and working with groups of parents that understand what it is like to feel hopeless and have come to be hopeful again. It's a risk of trusting other people who have been on the same journey. When you shed your pride and ego and find an addiction therapist or join a support group, you will find that it will also benefit your addicted son or daughter in a powerful way. Hope lingers even when we feel hopeless. It's up to you to take the first step to remove hopelessness and depression from your life.

You will recall the words of Solomon the wisest man who ever lived.

> There is a time for everything…a time to be born and a time to die, a time to plant and a time to uproot, a time to tear down and a time to build, a time to weep and a time to laugh, a time to mourn and a time to dance, a time to search and a time to give up, a time to keep and a time to throw away, a time to tear and a time to mend, a time to be silent and a time to speak, a time to love and a time to hate, a time for war and a time for peace. (Ecclesiastes 3:1–8, NIV)

Has self-pity pushed you into the pits?

It's easy for self-pity to creep into your life when you find out that your son or daughter is addicted to alcohol/drugs. You look around at your friends and their kids seem normal. They look happy while you feel sad and miserable most of the time. The hopes and dreams you had for your child have turned into fear and anxiety, causing you to dread life rather than looking forward to what each day has in store for you.

It has been said that envy is nothing more than a hostile form of self-pity. Self-pity can turn you into a victim with resentments toward others. To envy another person because you think they have what you want is a total waste of time. Indulging in self-pity will only create a downward spiral toward depression and despair. Will you succumb, or will you learn to rally yourself toward hope and happiness? It's up to you.

When you find yourself fixated on self-pity, a good practice to remember is to think about all that you are grateful for; make a grateful list. Create a list of all the gifts, talents, and abilities you have been given. This practice gives your mind time to free itself from the roadblocks that keep you stranded, preventing you from feeling happy. Learn to recognize when self-pity starts creeping into your thinking and identify it for what it is, a waste of time.

Why waste time thinking about what you're are not getting out of life and refocus your attention on what you do have, as well as what you can contribute to someone else's life? What can you give to help others in a healthy way where you can move beyond your problems and learn to give others unconditionally, receiving nothing in return? Every day can be an opportunity to change your life by helping others. When you discover how to make a positive contribution, large or small, you will be able to replace self-pity with self-esteem, depression with optimism.

> But as for me, my feet had almost slipped;
> I nearly lost my foothold. For I envied the
> arrogant when I saw the prosperity of the
> wicked. (Psalm 73:2–3, NIV)

Are you minding your mind?

You know the minute you wake up what kind of day it's going to be. Is your mind and spirit ready for this day? Sometimes you can wake up with a sick feeling in your stomachs, and it keeps on churning throughout the day. Other days you might feel stronger and ready to accomplish tasks and goals. Then there are those in-between days where you just seem to be in limbo, wondering about life and its purpose, its challenges and issues, especially addiction concerns.

Throughout your life, your mind and spirit can take a beating, especially if you are a parent of an addicted child. It's hard to keep negative thoughts and resentments from entering your mind. When you hold onto resentments and blame, your mind and spirit can spiral downward into a state of depression. However, you do have a choice on whether to entertain those negative thoughts and resentments.

Your thoughts dominate your attitude, as well as your day. Why not choose to start out our day with a positive thought. Blaming your attitude on outside circumstances can be a way of avoiding changes you need to make in yourself. You need to learn to be vigilant about your own recovery by taking responsibility for your own attitudes. When you take responsibility for your attitude, you are empowering yourself to elevate your mind and spirit, therefore finding a more nurturing way to treat yourself.

When you are faced with difficult and painful situations, you can choose to remember that your loving God is always there for you. The Bible is the best place to find words that will elevate your mind and spirit, instilling in you an awe of God's power and love.

James 1:2–3 (NIV) states,

> Consider it pure joy, my brothers, whenever you face trials of many kinds, because you know that the testing of your faith develops perseverance. Perseverance must finish its work so that you may be mature and complete, not lacking in anything.

Are you choosing to be a victim?

We can't pretend to understand what motivates another person's behavior or understand their circumstances. When we are depressed by our addicted child's behavior, problematic situations they are experiencing, or an upsetting turn of events, we need to remind ourselves that we do not have to take this personally. We are not victims unless we choose to be. As they say in the world of addiction, victims don't get well. Therefore, you need to understand your resentments that have built up recently or over the years and learn to forgive so that love has a chance to grow again in your own life.

When you blame others for the way you feel, you are giving them power over your feelings, as well as your life. Without your permission, no one can make you feel something you don't agree with. When you choose to use words such as, "You did this to me. You made me feel this way. You made my life miserable," you are choosing to stay in a victim's mentality rather than forgiving and letting go of old resentments that keep you from having what you want out of life. When you can talk about what you want out of life rather than continuing to hold on to past resentments and placing blame on others, you're choosing to no longer be a victim but a person who is capable of moving forward with your own personal growth and success, having an ability to love unconditionally.

Because of God's unconditional love, you know you are cared for and have great worth. Whoever believes will experience the love of God personally. Because of God's unsurmountable love, you will know and feel His love personally. People will see you believing in that love when they see the joy in your life and the strange absence of all prior resentments.

> Beloved, if God so loved us, we also ought
> to love one another. (1 John 4:11, NIV)

Is your life filled with distraction and disruption?

As parents of an addicted son or daughter, we are living in a world filled with distraction and disruption caused by our child's addiction to alcohol/drugs. The disruption comes and goes with peaks and lows, giving us the uneasy feeling of riding a roller coaster that does not seem to have an end. This distraction sometimes causes us to lose focus with our own lives. Our days begin and end with feelings of anxiety and depression, causing us to make illogical decisions rather than reasonable and sound ones.

Our child's addiction is punctuated with conflict that screams with drama, confusing our normal reasoning capabilities. You find yourself acting out of fear, making irrational decisions that will not have the outcome that you are so desperately seeking for yourself and your son or daughter. Distractions caused by addiction also "come upon you in a form and at a speed that does not allow you to process the content but only feel its impact. At times, you feel you do not know what hit you. You do not know what is happening to you, and this is precisely what is happening to you... not knowing what is happening to you."[21]

You must realize that this barrage can have a debilitating impact on your mental and spiritual well-being. It can blur your focus and color your frame of reference. Therefore, you must learn to turn to God in your hour of need. He is steadfast and all-knowing, and He can give you lucidity and peace of a sound mind, helping you make better decisions for yourself, as well as your addicted loved one.

> My son, pay attention to what I say; turn your ear to my words. Do not let them out of your sight, keep them within your heart; for they are life to those who find them and health to one's whole body. (Proverbs 4:20-22, NIV)

Are you sick and tired of being sick and tired?

When you experience a sense of despair in your everyday life with little interest in doing the things that you used to enjoy, depression is more likely setting in and can go from mild to severe depending on where you are in the cycle. Do you feel that you are spiraling downward with little hope things will change? Having a son or daughter with addiction issues can get the best of anyone. Consequently, you find yourself saying, "I'm sick and tired of being sick and tired."

In the medical field, this condition is called anhedonia. *Anhedonia* is a feeling of having little joy or interest in the things you used to love to do. You need to become aware of this condition because it can get the best of you if you don't reach out for help. When we are in desperate need of help, the first place we usually turn is the Word, the Bible, God's inspired message to all Christians. The book is about real people, with real problems looking to a real God for solutions. The Bible contains the secret sauce for spiritual growth.

Along with prayer and studying God's Word, you should look to other means for support on addiction issues as well, a good addiction counselor, group support, such as PAL or Al-Anon, and also reading good books on addiction, all of which are great resources for gaining knowledge.

Knowledge can be self-empowering whereas ignorance can be disempowering.

God leads us into the unknown—don't let the unknown keep you in the mundane. God gives us direction through the leading of the Holy Spirit. By following the Holy Spirit's lead, God teaches us to trust. Our human nature imparts a sense that we must be in control, making it difficult to turn our trust over to someone we cannot see or touch. You know God wants a personal relationship with you. Therefore it is your responsibility to cultivate that relationship. Since trust is the basic premise of a relationship, we should trust that he leads us by his peace and Holy Spirit. Move forward with your life by turning your life over to the will of God by developing a trusting relationship with him.

> May the God of Hope fill you with all joy
> and peace as you trust in him, so that you
> may overflow with hope by the power of
> the Holy Spirit. (Romans 15:13, NIV)

Are you having trouble keeping a positive attitude?

Because you are dealing with an addicted son or daughter, you probably are having a tough time keeping a positive attitude. Addiction issues can create a storm in your life, rearing its ugly head, generating a path of despair and destruction. Is it possible to have a positive attitude in the midst of such a storm?

It has been said that attitudes are nothing more than habits of thought, and habits can be acquired. You are what you are and what you are because of the dominating thoughts that occupy your mind. You first must form habits. Then habits form you. If you don't consciously form good habits while striving for a successful future, you will unconsciously form bad ones. It's just as easy to form the habit of succeeding as it is to succumbing to the habit of failure.

It is a psychological fact that we can influence our environment and thoughts. If we do so consciously and with high purpose, we can change our habits and attitudes for the better. The person who sets high goals and keeps a positive attitude inspires everyone around them. That person can be you, a person who climbs steadily and others follow.

Think of what I call the four big *D*'s to success: Desire, you have to want it. It can't be wished on you by someone else. Determination, nothing in life is ever smooth sailing, a bed of roses, so to speak. Problems and obstacles will always be there. Keep in mind that progress is two steps forward and one step back. Discipline, it takes self-control and restraint to achieve goals and maintain a positive attitude. Dedication, the act of committing yourself to something while maintaining enthusiasm. The level of commitment is directly parallel to the level of success. "Tough time's never last but tough people do" (Robert Schuller).

> Never be lacking in zeal, but keep your
> spiritual fervor, serving the Lord. Be joyful
> in hope, patient in affliction, and faithful
> in prayer. (Romans 12:11–13, NIV)

Are you letting fear and anxiety take control of your life?

Having a loved one with addiction issues can cause you to develop an enormous amount of anxiety and fear that can lead to depression if not kept in check. The Lord Jesus, again and again, exhorts believers to let go of all our anxiety and fears. How is that really possible?

When you first discovered your child had been affected by the destructive behaviors of substance abuse, the impact it had was probably the same as though your child had just died. Unfortunately, it's a moment in time when you realized that your addicted child will never be the same again and neither will you. However, the good news is that you can feel joy again, not letting the reality of your child's addiction destroy you.

The Lord says that you are powerless to change His plan or improve your circumstances by worrying over the details in your life, even your child! As a believer, you have a heavenly Father who knows your needs and concerns, promising to meet your needs. Are you tempted to say, "But I can't just sit and do nothing about my child's addiction problems." God is calling you to trust Him for all your troubles. He knows your needs and is aware of your concerns and wants you to trust his provision in every area of your life. Again and again, God encourages you to give up your anxiety and worry. What a relief it would be to let go of our fears and let God take over. As the Al-Anon slogan goes, "Let go and let God."

In the world of addiction, you can be continually tempted to worry, to wake in the night with the mental and emotional turmoil about your life and circumstances. Perhaps you need to be reminded once again to go to your heavenly Father in prayer and pour out your heart, to lay before Him all your mental and emotional agonies. He knows your every concern. You are His beloved.

> Do not be anxious about anything, but in everything by prayer and petition, with thanksgiving, present your requests to God. And the peace of God which transcends all understanding, will guard your hearts and your minds in Christ Jesus. (Philippians 4:6–7, NIV)

Has your adult child threatened suicide?

As a parent of a child with chemical dependency, you may worry about the possibility of suicide. Coming to terms with this possibility that addiction might take your child's life, you will naturally want to reach out and help. The healthy kind of help you offer may cause confusion and fear. Knowing your child is at high risk for death for a number of reasons, including disease, accident, and suicide, may give you pause as to how to deal with this risk. Suicide prevention requires a multifaceted approach, but all is dependent on your child reaching out for help and effective treatment being available when they do.

In some incidences, your adult child may tell you they are contemplating suicide. This could be a warning that they are in need of professional help; or they could be using it as a manipulation tool when they need something, perhaps money. The decision to help becomes complex when they are threating suicide, maybe even accusing you of not caring if you don't give them what they need.

In many situations, your child is desperate for drugs, so how do you know for sure when they ask for money that it will be going toward necessities like food or paying for the drugs that could kill them? The short answer is that you don't. Remember that we are dealing with adult children that have not developed good coping skills, turning to drugs/alcohol to self-medicate to try to avoid problems which may help in the short-term but exacerbate over time.

Suicide prevention begins with treatment. When your child is feeling self-destructive, first seek help to get professional advice. It is advisable that to help your adult child with suicidal thoughts/threats that they get a comprehensive psychiatric assessment to detect if there is a mental disorder along with their chemical dependency. A general practitioner can arrange or recommend a psychiatric assessment be done. In an urgent situation, the police can be called, or your child can be taken to a hospital emergency center.

Also, when your child talks about committing suicide, it may be that they have often felt like suicide, but they did not plan to carry out this self-destructive act immediately nor in the near future. Sometimes it can be a back-up plan if their situation were to get a lot worse. As parents, of course, we are haunted over the thought of our child taking their life. You should realize that you cannot decide for them whether their life is worth continuing or not. You cannot make the choice for them. They are adults and will make their own choices. By reminding them that you love them no matter what and reassuring them that you know they can beat this problem tells them you love them and support them in their fight for recovery.

> So do not fear, for I am with you; do not be dismayed, for I am your God. I will strengthen you and help you; I will uphold you with my righteous right hand. (Isaiah 41:10, NIV)

Chapter 6

Education
Understanding the Truth

Any fool can know... The point is to understand. (Albert Einstein)

Have you created a foundation of new knowledge?

As a parent who has an addicted son or daughter, you need to discover and understand things you didn't know you needed to learn. Dealing with your addicted child can be overwhelming and stressful. Your son or daughter will need to make many changes but so do you in order to cope. You will need to commit to reevaluating your own values, beliefs, habits, and behavior. Gaining as much knowledge on addiction and recovery is an important step for you as a parent to take so that you can begin healing and help your addicted child in their process for recovery.

Educational opportunities can be realized through books, counselors, and support groups. Your foundation of knowledge can be achieved in six to twelve months, if you are determined. It needs to be tackled with a long-term approach in mind, learning new things and putting them into practice. Change must happen, or the same cycles will repeat themselves.

The next step is to start setting goals for yourself. You need to understand that there are four basic types: short-term goals (two months to a year), long-term goals (one to five years), tangible goals (ones you can touch and feel), and intangible goals (what you want to become). In this situation, you are looking to set short-term goals. Make a list on paper rather than in your mind for each of these types. Remember, if you can't see your target, how can you hit it? Setting goals and meeting those goals gives you a boost in your self-esteem, your confidence. Otherwise, life can go off target too easily, and you end up somewhere else.

Why not start your short-term goal list with a good book on addiction or codependency. Make a call and find a support group, preferably for parents with an addicted child. Visit the Al-Anon.com website or the Palgroup.org website or Celebraterecovery.com for a support group near you and a list of good books. By doing this, you will be armed with a new awareness and new tools, a good foundation to help you navigate your way through the perils of having a child with substance abuse issues.

> Ask and it will be given to you; seek and you will find; knock and the door will be opened to you. For everyone who asks receives; the one who seeks finds; and to the one who knocks, the door will be opened. (Matthew 7:7–8,NIV)

Are you confused about treatment choices?

It's easy to get confused about the various options available for a son or daughter with chemical dependency.

This page will help you understand the choices that exist for helping your addicted son/daughter find sobriety.

Detox: this is not considered treatment but rather a dedicated amount of time, usually two to seven days, for the gradual removal of the addictive toxins from the body. The amount of time this takes is dependent on the age of the patient, how long they have been using, and how much they consume. This safe process is done in a controlled environment performed by nurses/doctors.

Residential treatment: this is an inpatient program (also known as rehab) designed for a specific period of time, anywhere from thirty days to six months. The patient is lodged for twenty-four hours a day, seven days a week. the patient is on a specific schedule every day with close monitoring of health issues, as well as participating in educational classes and individual/group therapy sessions.

Partial hospitalization (PHP): this treatment is part outpatient and part inpatient treatment. Usually six hours are spent at a treatment center, Monday to Friday, with the remaining hours a day at home or at a sober-living facility. A patient usually participates between one and four weeks in this treatment program.

Intensive outpatient treatment (IOP): the patient does not live at the treatment center in this program but commits to attending treatment activities that include education and group therapy two to three hours a day for three to four days a week. The length of this treatment is usually about eight weeks.

These various treatment options can be performed separately or in combination depending on the patient's needs and financial situation. Most of these treatment opportunities incorporate twelve-step programs such as Alcoholics Anonymous (AA), Narcotics Anonymous (NA), and Cocaine Anonymous (CA), etc.

> And the God of all grace, who called you to his eternal glory in Christ, after you have suffered a little while, will himself restore you and make you strong, firm and steadfast. (1 Peter 5:10, NIV)

Do you recognize the fine line between nurturing and crippling?

When you become a parent, nurturing is one of the most important components for raising your child. Young children's healthy growth involves loving and nurturing them to maturity. Although maturity should progress through childhood and adolescence, to adulthood and beyond, sometimes parents can get carried away with the nurturing component and forget about the importance of learning discipline and teaching "coping skills." When a parent doesn't give their child the freedom to make choices (good and bad) and accept the consequences of those choices, they enter into what we call "enabling" actions. Enabling behavior can cripple a child's emotional maturity.

As a parent, you will want to continue to do nice things for your son/daughter like cooking dinner or enjoying a football game together. You should not feel guilty about doing nice things for them up to a point. Sometimes this can be confusing because you don't want to reward bad behavior but rather good behavior. In the process of helping your addicted child, it is easy to fall into the pitfall of helping when it is doing just the opposite.

Before you can help your child, you must help yourself first. It's like when the flight attendant asks you to first put the air mask on yourself before helping your child put on their air-mask. You must take the first steps in your own recovery to be able to help your child in their recovery. The first step can be joining a support group, seeking individual counseling, and/or reading up on addiction. Sometimes a parent hesitates to get help because of the stigma that surrounds addiction. Perhaps you think that seeking help means that you have to admit your child has an alcohol/drug problem which can be difficult for parents to confess. Remember your son/daughter is not a bad or crazy person but rather using chemicals to feel better for deeper, less obvious mental issues. It's important and necessary for parents to gain an understanding of the disease because by helping yourself, you are helping your child. Family involvement increases the odds of improvement while helping maintain any positive gains.

> The words of the reckless pierce like swords, but the tongue of the wise brings healing. (Proverbs 12:18, NIV)

Does your addicted child have a co-occurring disorders?

Your child may be facing more than an addiction issue, having been diagnosed with other mental disorders such as anxiety, depression, bipolar disorder, PTSD and/or ADHD etc. Addiction professionals describe this as "co-occurring disorders" or "dual diagnosis." In many cases, it may be difficult to diagnosis which is the primary disorder (which came first) as they commonly go hand-in-hand, making it more difficult for parents to understand their child's struggles with addiction.

How do you know if your child has other mental issues that are making recovery difficult? A thorough initial assessment should be undertaken if you know or suspect a psychiatric issue has presented itself in your child. This can be critical to a person's ability to make long-term changes related to substance abuse. Remember medication is not a magic bullet but something that should not be avoided or feared if the assessment warrants pharmacotherapies. Find an addiction psychiatrist who can assess the psychiatric issues and recommend medication if needed.

Medications, along with therapy, can be powerful components in helping a person find sobriety. It's usually accepted that treatment should include pharmacotherapies if two or more mental disorders present themselves. Medication assisted recovery (MAR) is a new way to describe a pathway to recovery made possible by physician-prescribed and monitored medications, along with counseling and peer support. More and more treatment centers are including MAR principles with patients that have co-occurring disorders. It can be an important tool in the treatment for addiction.

Also, the doctor and counselor interaction when working with patients experiencing complex situations is critical to the success of treatment. Both treatment and medication should be done by cooperating professionals. It is essential that communication take place between the treatment team to create an optimal situation for the patient. If your child has been diagnosed with another mental disorder, pharmacotherapies can be an essential and crucial part of their recovery.

> The LORD himself goes before you and will
> be with you; he will never leave you nor

forsake you. Do not be afraid; do not be discouraged. (Deuteronomy 31:8, NIV)

How to empower the power of the Holy Spirit?

As a parent facing addiction in your child, you need to use every means to empower the Holy Spirit, giving up the right to control. When temptation comes your way to try and fix your addicted child's problems, lean into Christ, and He will guide your heart. The Bible tells us that our spiritual inheritance includes the Holy Spirit, faith and trust. There is a direct correlation between God's Word and the Holy Spirit in your effectiveness and enjoyment of the Christian life no matter what circumstances and hardships present themselves.

There are basic principles that can help you strengthen the power of the Holy Spirit that resides in you. When confronted with the knowledge that your son/daughter has an addiction to alcohol/drugs, remember and practice these important principles that will help strengthen the Holy Spirit in you, swallowing up the hopelessness you might be feeling.

Be grateful: when you're feeling sorry for yourself, make a grateful list. God loves a grateful believer.

Persevere: excellent lives do not just happen. It's up to us to takes God's promises as truth.

Obey: God commands us to obey, acting on God's Word and what he asks us to do.

Don't settle: we need each other, other believers that have walked in your shoes.

Wage war on sin: confess all sin to God, asking God to reveal all sin in our lives. Ask God to search your heart and purify a right spirit in you.

Believe: follow God wholeheartedly

Ask, seek, and knock: God will give us the desires of our heart. God gives us the desire to seek Him.

Read the Gospel: find a church, join a Bible study group, and seek out a good daily devotional to start your day.

Meditate: spend time in nature, using your five senses, listening to the sounds around you, enjoying the beauty of God's creation, and using the sense of smell, taste, and touch to enhance the process of meditation.

Listen to godly music: fill your mind with godly worship and praise through the medium of music.

Share your journey: your suffering and hope can give support and encouragement to others

Forgive: learn the art of forgiving yourself and others. Quit beating yourself and others up.

Just like the roots of an Oak tree, go deep into the earth, empowering it to hold steady in a storm in the same way the Holy Spirit fills us with God's power and gives us the strength to stand firm in our Christian faith when trials come into our life.

> And I will ask the Father, and he will give you another advocate to help you and be with you forever—the Spirit of truth. The world cannot accept him, because it neither sees him nor knows him. But you know him, for he lives with you and will be in you. (John 14: 16–17, NIV)

Do you know the early signs of relapse?

As a parent of a chemically addicted child, you may have experienced a period where your child gets their sobriety back, giving you a reprieve from the debilitating effects that you have experienced while your child was active in their addiction. It is not uncommon for a sober child to relapse, picking up a drink or drug again. There are normally many warning signs in a person's thinking, attitudes, relationships, feelings, and moods. In recovery, your addicted child will discover most of their triggers (sights, sounds, and smells). Knowing what these early warning signs are can help you see and understand a relapse is coming. Hopefully your child will ask you to watch for their warning signs in their behavior, emotions, or thinking as a form of accountability.

Your addicted child may experience a change in their thinking, including old patterns that reveal that they think they can control their drinking or drug use. Perhaps they start reminiscing about the good times, overlooking the problems connected with past substance abuse. Often a sober addict will use drinking/drug use as a reward for their success or a belief that they cannot succeed.

Your child's attitudes may also change as they move toward a relapse. Negative attitudes such as apathy, negativity, selfishness, and a belief that not drinking or using is an undeserved punishment may enter into the equation as they drift toward a relapse.

How your child is relating to others may slowly change. You may see your child slipping back into addictive patterns, such as isolation, manipulation, dishonesty, secretiveness, being resentful, and demanding, and putting their own wants and desires before others.

Some of the other addictive behavior patterns include having irregular eating and sleeping habits, neglect of health, irresponsibility, reckless high-risk behaviors, procrastination, impulsivity, and a loss of self-control. Common addictive patterns of feelings and moods include irritability, anxiety, self-pity, anger, and self-centeredness.

The salvation of the righteous comes from
the LORD; he is their stronghold in time

of trouble. The LORD helps them and delivers them; he delivers them from the wicked and saves them, because they take refuge in him. (Psalm 37:39–40, NIV)

What is transitional living and what is its value?

Transitional living is a choice of living accommodations that is available for a person who has completed a treatment plan. It is an option for a newly recovering person who may not have all the necessary coping skills necessary to deal with the challenges of life and the full responsibilities of independent living. Transitional living is a stage between the initial treatment for getting sober and independent living, providing time for adjustment from a twenty-four-hour structured treatment program to a less-structured-living accommodation. There are basically three choices for transitional living for the newly sober patient during this intermediate period: halfway house, three-quarter house, or sober-living housing. Each of these options offers a safe, supportive, hard to manipulate, and sober environment for the newly sober addict to grow and mature on their journey for a completely sober life.

Halfway house: while a person is taking advantage of the benefits of this half-step toward full independent living, they are expected to obtain low stress employment while paying affordable rent. This type of facility can be a large home with multiple rooms or an apartment with multiple units. In this structured environment, a newly sober person can benefit from a number of ways to spend their free time: visiting friends, seeing a counselor, going to AA meetings and house meetings, finding and working with a sponsor, making sober friendships, participating in fun recreational activities, developing their spirituality (church, Bible study, morning devotional time, etc.) Homes have full and part-time management that are there to oversee that the rules of participation are met, which may include drug testing, curfews, and perhaps attending a certain number of twelve-step meetings a week.

Three/quarter house: this is a generic term which implies less structure than a halfway house and fewer rules. This alternative also includes management who have less supervision and control. This choice depends on the maturity of its residents to provide the discipline to enforce the rules of the house.

Sober living house: another generic term used to describe a sober-living environment with fundamentally no structure, policy, or rules to follow. This is a situation where mature residents are simply looking for sober roommates. This flexible living structure has no management, solely depending on the maturity of its residents for a sober environment.

The most common length of stay in a transitional living facility varies from ninety days to a year. When a reentry plan is being developed, there are several factors to consider: how old is the person, how severe is there addiction, how long they have used, how many times they have been in treatment, the number of relapses, and has there been a period of clean and sober living. Transitional living is a good choice, giving the recovering person more time to adjust to a more independent and responsible way of life without the extra pressures of sober living while temporarily reducing the increased stresses and pressure of returning to their previous home after treatment.

Are you challenged with the lack of maturity in your adult child?

There is always an element of Delayed Emotional Growth in an alcoholic/addict. Mike Speakman, PAL founder, states in his book *The Four Seasons of Recovery*, "a short definition of Delayed Emotional Growth is a dysfunctional condition experienced by a child who has matured physically and intellectually but not psychologically, having difficulty coping with the normal stresses and responsibilities of adulthood."[22]

A common reason young and older adults turn to alcohol/drugs is that they have not learned to cope with life's problems and challenges. When a person turns to self-medication with drugs/alcohol to diminish their inability to deal with various difficult issues, they will stop maturing psychologically. The age you view your adult child is probably the age they started using drugs/alcohol to cope. So let's say your adult child is twenty-five, but you view him/her as fifteen; fifteen is probably the age they started abusing drugs/alcohol. Therefore, it should not be surprising that many alcoholic/addicts never realize the onus for their behavior lies with them because they were never prepared for adulthood.

Emotional growth will continue to occur as your adult child ages, except in the case of an addict. Emotional growth and maturity are stunted when your child is chemically dependent and will not move forward again until he/she is in recovery, free from substance abuse. As our culture changes, there seems to be fewer and fewer opportunities for children to learn about good decision-making. Perhaps one of the reasons is that parents are not letting their children experience the pain of poor decision-making. Parents have an instinctual tendency to protect children from painful situations; so they unintentionally overprotect, preventing a child from learning the natural way by experiencing suffering and pain from their mistakes. However, the good news is that it is never too late to start this practice, especially when your child is in the throes of addiction.

> These commandments I give you today are
> to be upon your hearts. Impress them on
> your children. (Deuteronomy 6:6–7, NIV)

What role does each member of your family play?

As parents of an addicted son or daughter, you should be familiar on how the family system works and what roles each family member will play in a typical home with an addicted child. Because the family usually needs to adapt to the person that abuses drugs/alcohol, each member will take on a different role that helps reduce the stress from the insecurity the chemically dependent child triggers. The rest of the family is trying to cope with the craziness and uncertainty of the addicted family member so these roles are unconsciously adopted for survival because each family member believes that they are reducing the stress prompted by the addicted member. Although these roles can reduce stress, they do not reduce anxiety. Anxiety can eventually cause mental and behavioral disorders. These roles include the enabler, the hero, the scapegoat, the lost child, and the mascot.[23]

The enabler is the family member who steps in and protects the alcoholic/addict child from the consequences of their bad behavior. This person believes they are protecting the alcoholic/addict, preventing embarrassment, reducing anxiety, avoiding conflict, or trying to maintain control of a tough situation. This family member will try to make excuses and clean up the mess caused by the addicted family member.

The hero is the family member who will attempt to draw attention away from the addicted son or daughter or sibling. This member of the family tries hard to be the perfect child, excelling and performing exceptionally well. This family member hopes that their behavior will have a positive effect for change on the alcoholic/addict. The hero's performance-based behavior helps them to block emotional pain caused by the chemically dependent person.

The scapegoat is a family member who will create other problems and issues in order to deflect attention away from the real issue. This family member may use misbehavior, bad grades, or indulge in substance abuse themselves.

The lost child is a family member who comes across as unaware of the problem. When there is an argument, screaming, or fighting, this family member will go into seclusion, absent from the situation, avoiding personal stress. The lost child is often perceived as the "good" child because they have learned to distract themselves with a book or social media.

The mascot: this family member tries to use humor as a method to escape the pain of problems caused by addiction. They are often seen "clowning around," cracking jokes, and making light of a serious situation. They try to lighten up a desperate situation, easing tension and trying to keep peace.

These role descriptions don't fit an exact mold but come close to describing the family system dynamics when there is an addicted family member. These roles are developed for survival.

> Train up a child in the way he should go; even when he is old he will not depart from it. (Proverbs 22:6, NIV)

Do you understand how "defense mechanisms" work?

As a parent of a son or daughter addicted to alcohol/drugs, you have more than likely encountered many stressful situations if not insane conditions, situations that can push you to the breaking point of what you can tolerate. Your brain protects you from these stressful situations using "defense mechanisms." These "defense mechanisms" contribute to your mental health by providing relief from stress that can plague you while you're dealing with all the drama that comes with having an addicted loved one.

Sigmund Freud's daughter, Anna Freud, described ten different defense mechanisms used by the ego. Other researchers have also described a wide variety of additional defense mechanisms. Here is a list of some of the most frequently used "defense mechanisms" and an explanation of how they work:

Denial: a person, parent, or addicted child that refuses to accept reality

Rationalization: uses excuses to try and justify one's actions

Repression: unconsciously holding back feelings by using distractions

Projection: blaming others in an attempt to protect your feelings or self-esteem

Suppression: consciously holding back feelings and thoughts because you see it as a sign of weakness

Compensation: excelling in certain areas to compensate for weakness in another

Sublimation: finding acceptable behavior to cover up unacceptable behavior

Reaction formation: acting or functioning in opposition to what you feel

Conversion: stress and emotional problems result in physical disorders

Regression: acting as if you were back in an earlier trouble-free time

Identification: modeling behaviors after a person you like

Escape or fantasy: running away from stress and issues through daydreaming, books, or sleeping excessively.

Hopefully, these "defense mechanisms" can help you understand how the disease of addiction can affect you, as well as your addicted son or daughter. Your child will use these, as well as you. Everyone has them, but addicts use them to maintain their addiction. Please realize that dependence on them can lead to the real issue of avoidance, inability of facing your and your loved one's problems.

> For the word of God is alive and active. Sharper than any double-edged sword, it penetrates even to dividing soul and spirit, joints and marrow; it judges the thoughts and attitudes of the heart. (Hebrews 4:12, NIV)

What is the level of your child's motivation to change?

Your child's level of motivation to change is frequently a good predictor on whether your son or daughter will change and want sobriety. The ability for your child to be ready, willing and able to freely make a desired behavioral change, is key in their capacity for a successful recovery. Motivation along with a willingness and ability to change all belong to your addicted child. These can be enhanced or diminished by interactions with family, friends, and others along with events in his/her life. The task of a parent, family member, professional counselor, sponsor, or other professional is to help your child find the internal motivation to change.

As you may already know, not all addicts entering into addiction treatment accept they have a problem. Many are not ready to discontinue their use of alcohol/drugs. Many professionals use the "stages of change model" when taking into consideration various treatment options. Prochaska and DiClemente developed this process which focuses on the decision-making of the individual where change occurs continuously. In this process, five distinct stages are recognized. These stages represent responsibilities and experiences that the addict undertakes as they make behavioral changes: precontemplation, contemplation, preparation, action, and maintenance.

Precontemplation: during this stage of change, your child is not considering a need for change and is therefore uninterested in seeking help.

Contemplation: in this stage, your child is aware of the personal consequences of their addiction and spends time thinking about their problem.

Preparation: in this stage, your child has made a commitment to make a change.

Action: in the action stage, your child believes they have the ability to change and are actively involved in taking steps in recovery.

Maintenance/recovery: in this stage, your child learns to successfully avoid triggers/temptations that would lead back to active addiction.

By understanding your child's personal reasons for change along with allowing them to choose their path to recovery, you will be in a better position to help them make the necessary behavioral changes, maintaining long-term sobriety.

> No discipline seems pleasant at the time, but painful. Later on, however, it produces a harvest of righteousness and peace for those who have been trained by it. (Hebrews 12:11, NIV)

Are you familiar with the acronym PAWS?

Most alcoholics/addicts who decide to enter a treatment program need to go through a detoxification program before being admitted. *Detox* is a safe process, using various medications to help clean the toxins from the patient's body while keeping the patient as comfortable as possible. It is an inpatient/hospitalization program overseen by skilled nurses and a doctor. It is critical that a person not try and detox themselves from the substances they have been abusing because it can be life-threatening, as well as indescribably difficult. Detox can most likely take anywhere from three to seven days depending on how long a person's been drinking, the level of their addiction and their age.

Unfortunately, the end of detox will not mean the end to withdrawal. After the patient has been through detox and continues to stay clean and sober, the patient will continue to experience some degree of post-acute-withdrawal syndrome (PAWS). Each individual will be affected differently with a wide range of symptoms. The severity of PAWS will depend again on how long the patient has been abusing alcohol/drugs, the level of their addiction, their age, and how much damage was done to their nervous system. "Most experience PAWS immediately after detox with symptoms peaking at about 3 to 6 months. However, some patients have experienced PAWS for 2 or more years."[24]

PAWS can be described by the symptoms that the patient will experience while continuing to stay clean and sober. The patient will probably have difficulty with clear thinking (thought fog) such as concentration, problem solving, and processing their thoughts. Difficulty with managing or coping with stress (irritability) is another common symptom of PAWS. The patient could have difficulty in managing their emotions resulting in depression, feeling numb or sadness and anxiety. Also symptoms of difficulty with memory and ability to focus will more than likely surface. Knowing how PAWS works will help you cope with your child's erratic behavior during their recovery.

> For God hath not given us the spirit of timidity, but of a spirit of power, of love, and of self-discipline. (2 Timothy 1:7, NIV)

How long does it take to educate yourself on parenting an addicted child?

The answer depends on your own attitude, a willingness to make changes in yourself. Yes, I said changes you need to make for yourself. You have already learned the three C's (Al-Anon slogan): you can't change your chemically dependent child. You can't control him/her; and you sure can't cure your child. They need to make the choice to change themselves. The only thing you can do to help is motivate their desire to change, changing how you react and support them.

Your willingness to make changes in your self is totally up to you and can only be measured by you. Some parents jump right in because of their despair and desire to find serenity in their life again. Others are reluctant because change isn't easy. You could say that your willingness and level of motivation to change can be measured using the same "five stages of change" as your addicted adult child.

Precontemplation: you are not considering a need to change and are therefore uninterested in gaining knowledge on addiction nor seeking help to change.

Contemplation: you are aware and thinking of the need to make some changes in the way you support and react to your addicted son/daughter.

Preparation: you are taking the steps to make changes in yourself, ready to join a support group, seek professional help, and gain knowledge on addiction.

Action: now you believe you can make changes that will help and benefit your addicted child and are taking the steps toward your own recovery.

Maintenance/recovery: you have learned how to set boundaries and stop your enabling behavior toward your son/daughter.

Change takes courage and strength. Your active substance abuser child doesn't drink/drug because of you but because they are alcoholics/addicts. No matter what you do, you will not change this fact, not with lecturing, guilt, begging, hiding money or bottles, lying, threatening, or trying to reason. When you accept this fact, you can begin the journey for your own recovery, as well as learn basic principles for change in you that will become a force for good that will help the entire family, including your chemically dependent child.

> Brothers and sisters, stop thinking like
> children…but in your thinking be adults.
> (1 Corinthians 14:20, NIV)

Are you constantly being put between a rock and a hard place?

Your chemically addicted son or daughter has probably become a pro at manipulation. Perhaps it's gone unnoticed, or maybe you have become aware of how easily you are talked into doing something that you later regret. Manipulation is a strategy used frequently when a person becomes dependent on alcohol and drugs. This acquired trait is used to deflect questions or to obtain something of benefit or assistance.

Children learn this trait early on, so is it any surprise when they continue this behavior into their adult years? A child quickly gets used to a parent jumping in to help rather than learning to deal with problems and issues themselves. Taking responsibility, no matter how trivial the problem may be, is an adult coping skill. Adult coping skills are often avoided when a person is avoiding change or the willingness to grow up, especially when parents are more than willing to step in and handle the situation.

According to Mike Speakman, the following are a list of adult coping skills: "being honest, earning your own money (legally), keeping commitments, submitting to authority, delaying gratification/being patient; accepting the answer no without taking it personally; giving up control when it is best to do so; making responsible decisions; recognizing the good ones and learning from the bad ones; accepting responsibilities for all decisions; limiting selfishness; limiting unselfishness."[25]

In an addicted adult child who has not learned adult coping skills, it is often easier to revert to manipulation to get what they want or need. Parents are usually the best target because they are in the habit of helping when the need arises. And remember, your addict child will most likely make it sound like a crisis. Manipulation is often done when it is least expected. You, as a parent, are often caught off guard, responding too quickly to the pressure to help when you haven't had time to think about the request. Making your son or daughter wait on purpose for a response is a healthier way of handling it. Mike Speakman says, "No instant answer."[26] Tell them you'll think about it and get back to them.

As a child grows into adulthood and parents are still stepping in to help, the value of gaining self-esteem is lost. Self-esteem and confidence is nurtured by success as well as failure. These are good lessons for parents who feel the need to always lend a helping hand. Give yourself time to think about requests. It may take some practice to learn this new habit; but if you are consistent, your loved one will benefit, as well as you, taking away unwanted stress.

> But solid food is for the mature, who by constant use have trained themselves to distinguish good from evil. (Hebrews 5:14, NIV)

Did you know that there are several roles an addict can play?

According to several sources, the addicted child also adopts certain roles in order for them to survive while continuing their substance abuse. Here are some common roles:

Intimidator: uses anger and fear to drive people away

Intellectual: mistakes knowledge for understanding and good common sense

Victim: blames other people and negative events for their addiction

Avoider: will try to keep a low profile, trying to stay secluded as much as possible

Socialite: keeps a high profile but is superficial

Con person: thinks he or she is fooling everyone

Know it all: the expert and no one can tell them what they need to do

Magic fixer: thinks they know what caused their addiction and therefore can fix it

Skeptic: will take a good idea and tell you it won't work

Deflector: will try and focus attention away from themselves

Lip service: agrees to follow through but never does

Controller: will always try and control the course of their own recovery

Rabble rouser: likes to stir up conflict between people or groups

Paranoid: is distrustful and suspicious about giving out information or confiding with others

Your chemically dependent child will use these roles in order to try and deflect from their substance abuse. Addictive roles become important tools for your child in their attempt to manipulate you, as well as cope with their addiction. Understanding these predictable roles your son/daughter may misuse in order to get what they want helps you realize the dysfunction you are falling into. You need to respond in more healthy ways. The more you understand the roles of your addicted son or daughter can play, the harder it will be for him/her to control and manipulate you. When they no longer can control or manipulate you, they will begin to recognize and comprehend the need for professional help for their chemical dependency.

> Finally, be strong in the Lord and in his
> mighty power. (Ephesians 6:10, NIV)

Could you be experiencing withdrawal symptoms too?

Withdrawal is different for every addict or parent. For most addicts, it can be difficult, painful, and dangerous. When your child has been using chemicals daily, their brain will discern when the chemical has been discontinued, causing a withdrawal phenomenon that can manifest symptoms ranging from mild mood swings, including restlessness, irritability, to severe mood changes such as insomnia, depression, paranoia, seizures, and tremors.

For parents, withdrawal can be difficult too although it didn't originate from the use of chemicals but rather from chemical changes that take place in the brain caused from fear and a feeling of being out of control, manifesting itself with similar symptoms as the addict. When a parent initially finds out about their child's addiction, it can throw them into a tailspin, sending them into what feels like a dark bottomless pit.

For your addicted child, there are two stages of withdrawal, the acute stage and the post-acute stage. During the acute stage, the addict will experience physical withdrawal symptoms manifesting itself in a variety of ways, depending on the drug and person. During the second stage of withdrawal (post-acute withdrawal symptoms), the symptoms are less physical and more emotional and mental.

For a parent, there can also be a physical, as well as emotional and psychiatric withdrawal. The difference between an addicted child and parent is that the emotional and psychiatric symptoms will precede the physical. Emotional and psychiatric symptoms can bring on enough stress that will manifest itself in bad health. Post-acute symptoms for both the child and parent feel like a rollercoaster of symptoms that will change minute to minute and hour to hour.

As a parent of a chemically addicted child, you probably find yourself confused as well as being in a state of shock. You are slowly learning what a complex problem you and your child are facing. Because you have never been part of this life experience before, the psychiatric terms and the so-called lingo of addiction and rehab can cause fear and anxiety. When you find yourself experiencing withdrawal symptoms such as mood swings, anxiety, irritability, tiredness, a loss of energy, lack of enthusiasm, insomnia, and loss of concentration, you need to talk to your doctor/psychiatrist, a counselor, join a support group, and find good addiction books to educate yourself. Knowledge is power!

> And after you have suffered a little while,
> the God of all grace, who has called you
> to his eternal glory in Christ, will himself
> restore, confirm, strengthen, and establish
> you. (1 Peter 5:10, ESV)

What changes take place in the addicted brain?

Having a better understanding of what happens in the brain when addiction occurs is important for parents to understand if they have a son or daughter battling addiction. This brief summary will attempt to give you a simple explanation to this complex question. Some understanding of neurotransmitters and brain functioning can help you respond in a helpful way to your child's mood, cravings, and behaviors. First of all, addiction is not defined by whether your child can stop without the shakes, nausea, vomiting, aches, and pain. A person who binges regularly may not have signs of physical withdrawal but is putting themselves at risk for overdose with each binge. Addiction therapists frequently use the saying, "Addiction is the only disease that needs to be self-diagnosed."

People metabolize addictive substances differently. Your child's system can metabolize the addictive substance faster, slower, or not well at all. Also, their genetic makeup/inheritance can steer how they react to mind-altering substances, as well as how it effects the reward system in their brain. Differences in emotions about life, along with novelty seeking, risk seeking, and impulsivity, can possibly contribute to an increased risk of substance abuse. Research shows if a person is genetically predisposed, a person's propensity for addictiveness can generally be shown to be between 50%–60%.[27] The environment, social factors such as childhood abuse or neglect, trauma, loss of a parent and poor parent-child relations have a cause/effect on a person, as well as the culture has an impact on an individual's vulnerability.

Neuroscientists are teaching us that in the more than fifty neurotransmitters in the brain, the dopamine transmitter largely contributes to the areas of substance use. The dopamine receptor's job is to make you feel good, so naturally you want more of it. It's the brain's way of rewarding you. The brain calls for dopamine levels to rise and spike during pleasurable activity to ensure they do it again and again. The use of drugs/alcohol turns on a rush of dopamine in the brain, making a person feel really good, even euphoric, pushing out their natural dopamine. When the brain is flooded with dopamine repeatedly, it creates long-term effects and what we term *tolerance*. Tolerance is when your child loses their ability to produce or absorb their own natural dopamine, creating an artificial need for more and more addictive substance to fill the void. When natural production of dopamine is taken away by the addictive substance, there is not enough natural dopamine left to give pleasure. This means that they will not have the ability to enjoy anything. Lower levels of dopamine will cause cravings, a need to artificially raise their dopamine level by means of alcohol/drugs.

Substance abuse also affects the parts of the brain called the prefrontal cortex and limbic system. The prefrontal cortex shuts down when addictive substances flood the brain. On the other hand, the limbic system controls our sense of drive and urgency which is generated from our motivation, emotions, and memories. With substance abuse, this part of the brain becomes hyperactive, anticipating the reward of using along with the decision-making and judgmental prefrontal cortex more or less disabled, allowing a person to move forward with the impulse to use. Like the cravings from low dopamine levels, the hyperactive limbic system is also an automatic physiological process taking place unconsciously, without thinking.

Understanding the brain's role in substance use can help you feel more compassionate about your child's abuse of chemicals, as well as give you optimism about the potential for the brain to eventually recover. Understanding what your addicted child is going through can perhaps make it a bit more bearable for you. A good video for parents to watch is *Pleasures Unwoven*.[28]

> "I have the right to do anything," you say—but not everything is beneficial. "I have the right to do anything"—but I will not be mastered by anything. (1 Corinthians 6:12, NIV)

What is effective communication with your addicted child?

Communicating with your child is sometimes challenging, especially when chemical abuse is in the picture. But like any communication between individuals, there are certain basics that need to take place: As a parent of an addicted child, you will need to stick with these basics, always remembering to (1) stay focused, (2) listen carefully, (3) try to see your child's point of view, (4) respond, don't react to criticism, (5) look for compromise, (6) take a time out, (7) not give up.

Staying focused: try to not discuss past hurts, causing the discussion to be more taxing and perhaps confusing. It's best to stay focused on the present, your feelings, respecting one another so that you can come to a mutual understanding.

Listen carefully: ask your child what is wrong, really listening to their answer. They need to have the freedom to vent their fears and frustrations, feeling heard and understood. Please resist the need to give them advice. Trust this process. After your child has finished discussing their feelings, then you can start discussing solutions.

Try to understand their point of view: when you really try to understand their point of view, then you can better explain yours. Your child may be a person who overgeneralizes, taking isolated events and assuming all future events will be the same. They could also tend to gloss over positive events, emphasizing the negative. Sometimes a person clings to a more negative world, always seeing the glass half empty rather than half full. Sometimes, your child may want to jump to conclusions rather than looking at facts that support another conclusion. Also, it would be better for parents to avoid "should" statements because they come across as too rigid and not open-minded. Labeling people can also come across as being closed-minded.

Respond to criticism with empathy: don't get defensive when your child criticizes you even though it may be difficult to hear. It is better to respond with empathy for their feelings and look for things that might be true. If tempers get heated and it's impossible to continue without both of you yelling, it is better to break and walk away until tempers cool off.

Look for compromise: parents should not be bent on winning the argument rather looking for solutions that meet both of your needs. Healthy communication means finding answers and solutions that both of you can be happy with. If you and your child have problems staying respectful, it would be wise to look for a therapist. A therapist can keep the conversation on track, bringing resolution to differences.

Last but not least, don't give up! Words can hurt, or they can encourage. They can teach, or they can tear down. But no matter what, they are very powerful. They are also a huge reflection of what is in our heart. Learning to create an adult relationship with your child can be challenging, but the results will be rewarding for both of you.

> Let the words of my mouth and the meditation of my heart be acceptable in your sight, O LORD, my rock and my redeemer. (Psalm 19:14, NIV)

Do you know how to cope with your child's lying?

You are not alone with your struggles to understand that lying has now become a common characteristic in your addicted son or daughter. Because of the disease your child is battling, a parent soon realizes that lying is not unusual. It is a way of life that has become normal. The lies maybe blatant, or perhaps your addicted child will purposely omit information to try and deceive you. Lying is one of the frustrations that you may face even though your heart wants to believe everything they say. In the past. when communicating with your child, lying was probably not a factor until alcohol/drugs entered the picture. But now it is. There is a saying amongst addiction counselors that "if their mouth is moving, they are probably lying." Lying seems to be an integral part of addiction.

Lying is something that we all are guilty of at some point in our lives, trying to mitigate negative reactions in others, so we change the story or leave out pertinent facts. Because of your child's addiction, their brain is telling them they cannot survive without their drug of choice, so they will probably not be honest when you ask them if they are using drugs. Telling you the truth will force them into a corner where they will have to admit what's going on. If your child feels backed into a corner, they will probably choose to be dishonest. Confrontation is usually not helpful because it forces your child to lie their way out, feeling more shame and guilt and covering up what your child is perhaps is too ashamed to admit.

When your child's brain has been hijacked by drugs, it prevents them from being honest and truthful, compromising most of their behavior in a negative way. As a parent, you can usually forget about your addicted child having the ability to be honest. Your child's brain loses the capacity to be honest, reasonable, and insightful, affecting their ability to use moral values as a guiding compass for finding their way back to a clean and sober life.

Rather than forcing your child to lie, try and take the time to understand the motives behind their behavior. It will be easier for your child to be more truthful with you if you use a compassionate approach rather than a disciplinary one. As you know, your child's lying can be exhausting, as well as frustrating. It will be better for you to focus on their positive behavior, using compassion over judgement. Learn to talk to your child in a way that encourages truth-telling. The honesty you get with your child will depend on the approach you use.

> Do not let any unwholesome talk come out of your mouths, but only what is helpful for building others up according to their needs, that it may benefit those who listen. (Ephesians 4:29, NIV)

Chapter 7

Adjust
Focus on the Truth

If you don't like something, change it. If you can't change it, change your attitude. (Maya Angelou)

Do you really want to be on this journey alone?

Parents of an addicted son or daughter can find themselves somewhere between heaven and hell. Some days feel like a living hell, and other days seem pretty normal. When addiction is in the picture, there are more days feeling like hell than you ever thought you could imagine. These are the days when we need to place our hope and trust in the Lord.

Once, I heard a true story about a mountain climber who attempted to climb Mount Everest with only a single Sherpa guide. His name is Brian Dickerson. They were one day from reaching the top of the mountain when the Sherpa became ill and had to turn back. Because Brian had worked so hard to get in shape mentally and physically for this climb, he decided to push on by himself. He finally reached the top of the mountain only to find that his oxygen tank had failed. Mountain climbers train for thin air but never too this degree. Breathing becomes almost impossible. As he started his descent, about four hours from the top of the mountain, he started to lose his eyesight. Soon he found that he could no longer see. Feeling the sickening feeling of defeat, he almost gave in to the mountain. As his thoughts turned to God, he said this prayer, "God, I can't do this alone. Please help me."[29] The next thing he did was grab the oxygen tank and try it again. This time, it worked without a glitch. With the oxygen tank, he was able to make the only blind descent off Mount Everest in the history of mountain climbing. With the help of God leading him, he made history. It took him about a month to regain his full sight.

The reason I tell you this story is that sometimes God allows us to be pulled and stretched before he reaches out to help us. So I ask you as you struggle with the issues and challenges of your child's addiction, is God testing your faith and trust? When the oceans rise and fall, will you say, "I will be still and know that you are God?" Desperation can sometimes precede God's leading. Desperation might be a divine call from God. He wants to know if you can have faith and trust in him during desperate times or if you're just a fair-weather believer.

> Trust in the Lord with all your heart and lean not on your own understanding. In all your ways submit to him, and he will make your paths straight. (Proverbs 3:5–6, NIV)

Are you paying attention to your own health?

We must always keep in mind that our health is the most valuable asset that we have, so we must protect it as we do our other valuable assets. When you have a child that is addicted to alcohol/drugs, your own health can become secondary to theirs. While your son or daughter was growing into adulthood, you put the needs of your child ahead of yours, as you should. There was only so much time in a day, and much of it was spent caring and nurturing your child's needs, sometimes to the detriment of your own health.

You cannot help others as long as you do not take care of yourself. There's no halfway process that works. Your health can go downhill pretty quickly when you are not paying attention to little warning signs which give rise to clues that you are not taking care of yourself the way you should. Everyone has been through cycles when their body breaks down, falling victim to an illness, creating difficulty in caring for others while we are recovering.

Stress can be the main culprit in falling victim to an unhealthy lifestyle. The stress that an addicted child can bring on a parent can cause you to forget about your own well-being, focusing solely on your son or daughter's situation and challenges. A healthy lifestyle should include exercise, good nutrition, fun activities, and spiritual food, along with daily prayer.

Realize that each parent getting help for themselves is giving a gift to their addicted child. Part of your own recovery will ultimately help your addicted child. As a loving parent, you must move ahead with your own recovery regardless of your son or daughter's choices. Both parent and child need to seek freedom from the bondage that drugs/alcohol have caused in their lives. Your child's survival depends somewhat on the choices that you make during these struggles and the trials that addiction has brought your way.

> Do you not know that your body is a temple of the Holy Spirit, who is in you, whom you have received from God? You are not your own; you were bought at a price. Therefore honor God with your body. (1 Corinthians 6:19, NIV)

Are you giving up on your dreams for yourself and your addicted child?

Addiction in your son or daughter can put a damper on the dreams you had for them. From the minute they were born, you started to dream of the possibilities for your child. Unconditional love for your child can sometimes cause your own dreams to take a back seat to your dreams for your child. No matter what the circumstances, dreams should always be part of your life, as well as your addicted child's life. Don't let life get in the way of those dreams. Addiction happens but so does recovery.

Having an addicted child should not get in the way of having an exciting job, a new car, or taking an exciting trip to somewhere you have always dreamed. These are not impossible dreams. Whatever you want, you can bring about for yourself through goal setting. The single difference between a successful person and an unsuccessful person is that one achieves their goals and the other does not.

Without goals, you simply respond to situations in your environment as they occur, such as addiction. Using goals as a tool, you create situations that shape your environment. Your chances of achieving what you want are far greater when you are in control—when you know where it is you want to go, what is required of you, and how long it will take to get there.

We all have our reasons for being reluctant to set goals. To get behind your reluctance, you first need to identify the reasons for it, weigh their importance with that of the goal itself, and then resolve those reasons so that you can start shaping your life. Having an addicted son or daughter is not a reason to put off your goals. In fact, in makes it that much more important that you continue setting goals. Your adult child will need to make their own set of goals, making sobriety and a plan for sobriety their first priority.

So continually examine what is important to you in life and set goals to achieve it. It doesn't make sense to carry around goals that no longer reflect who you are and want to become. As you and society change, so will your values and lifestyles. Your goals must change too. Goals are the key to professional success and personal fulfillment. Don't procrastinate. Start your list. Make it a work in progress.

> May he give you the desire of your heart
> and make all your plans succeed. (Psalm
> 22:4, NIV)

What age do you visualize your addicted child?

According to Mike Speakman, "No matter what your child's biological age, parents visualize them at what they feel their emotional age is."[30] For example, when you close your eyes and see your son or daughter, what is their age that first comes to mind?

This exercise helps you to see your child at an age of their emotional maturity. When your son or daughter starts using drugs, they get stuck, unable to mature emotionally. By winning and losing at various challenges, a normal person grows emotionally together with their biological age. An addicted child does not.

Instead of using adult coping skills to solve problems and challenges, addicted children turn to drugs to help them cope rather than developing life's coping skills through life's experiences. They take the easy way out, so to speak. The feeling of failure looms above them as they try to cope with life's problems. So rather than push through their anxieties and fears, they turn to drugs/alcohol. The addicted son or daughter turns away from learning to cope, leaning on drugs/alcohol rather than figuring out the best answer to their situation and circumstance. Taking drugs is an easy way to temporarily fix the problem by blocking out feelings. The problem becomes temporarily removed from their mind. When using drugs and alcohol as a Band-Aid to coverup issues and problems, it can become a bad habit.

As a parent, you must become aware of their immaturity and stunted emotional growth, becoming willing to ask yourself: what is my part in this situation? Most of the time, you have been fixing problems and issues for them, taking away opportunities for them to learn from natural consequences that present themselves. Yes, pain from natural consequences can be hard to witness for a parent, but knowing that we are stunting their chance for emotional growth can be even more painful. It's time to help move forward your child's emotional growth clock and let them learn how to be a responsible, independent adult.

> If anyone thinks he is something when he is nothing, he deceives himself. Each one should test his own actions. Then he can take pride in himself, without comparing himself to somebody else, for each one should carry his own load. (Galatians 6:3–6, NIV)

Do you support your chemically addicted child by not drinking when you are with them?

It can be helpful to your addicted son or daughter in their early recovery if you don't drink in front of them. Some may say that "it is not your problem, so why do you need to stop drinking in the presence of your child?" The answer is simple to understand. Your addicted child has several triggers that can cause a relapse. Watching others drink can be a huge trigger even if alcohol is not their drug of choice. The first year is the most critical time of their recovery. As a parent with an addicted child, it is important to give as much support as humanly possible while they are in the first year of recovery.

Some parents stop drinking completely when their child has substance abuse issues. A parent can be a great source of encouragement. Although encouragement can come in many forms, staying sober in the presence of your child can be seen as a huge visual act of love and understanding. It says that you know sobriety is not easy, and you want to help and support in any way you can. Your child has taken the time and effort to change; so doesn't it make sense that you, as a parent, learn about things you can change to be supportive?

During family gatherings, it can be very helpful to limit drinking. Some ideas include keeping drinks in a generic cup because wine glasses and beer bottles can be a trigger. Maybe just having a few volunteers that would choose to stay sober would be enough encouragement without placing guilt or culpability on the one family member trying to get sober.

Today's society pushes alcohol in an effort to make it look as appealing and desirable as possible. Standing up to the temptations from big name advertisers can require a lot of inner strength from your child who is trying to stay sober. The more you can be supportive to your child's sobriety by not having alcohol at the front and center of every family function is a wise and compassionate decision.

The Father of compassion and the God
of comfort, who comforts us in all our

troubles, so that we can comfort those in any trouble with the comfort we ourselves have received from God. (2 Corinthians 1:4)

Why avoid the top floor of the hope hotel?

The "hope hotel" is a metaphor Mike Speakman uses for parents who need a reminder about controlling their recovery expectations for their addicted child.[31] When your chemically dependent son or daughter is doing well with their progress in a recovery program, you may find yourself on the top floor of the "hope hotel." Addiction counselors will remind you that the higher you are, the further you have to fall when your child relapses or isn't following their recovery program.

So again, you are reminded that you have no control over whether your child relapses or not. However, you can control how high your expectations are set, staying aware of what "hope hotel" floor you find yourself on. When you realize your hopes and expectations are probably too high, you need to get on the elevator, so to speak, and move down closer to the ground floor. It will be much less painful to fall one floor than to fall twenty-plus floors.

As a parent of an addicted child, you should always use caution in setting your expectations for your child's recovery too high. Even though the prospects for your child's recovery look very good, it is always a good idea to be "cautiously optimistic." By not assuming everything is going to be "smooth sailing" from here on out, you will be able to handle the emotional roller-coaster ride from the ups and downs that are associated with most recoveries. When your child relapses, it does not mean they have failed but is rather the next step in gaining self-knowledge for understanding what triggers their desire to abuse drugs. You can remind yourself that their recovery process is not a "sprint but rather a marathon." Addiction is a complex disease that affects your child's complex brain. Therefore, undoing the damage that has occurred physically, mentally, and spiritually will take time. The amount of time it will take cannot be controlled by you. "Let go and let God" (Al-Anon slogan). Prayer for patience is needed!

> Therefore, as God's chosen people, holy and dearly loved, clothe yourselves with compassion, kindness, humility, gentleness and patience. (Colossians 3:12, NIV)

Can you thrive again and turn pain into purpose?

Being a parent of a chemically addicted child can be an exhausting and grueling experience that can take away your vitality for life. Life can be difficult enough without adding addiction into the equation. Seeing your child gradually submit to the stranglehold of powerful drugs/alcohol can be the worst experience of your life. It can leave you feeling powerless and defenseless, unable to cope, let alone thrive. Dealing with the pain of watching your child make poor choices along with the consequences of those choices can leave you so frustrated that you begin to lose your way, losing sight of your own God-given purpose.

Resilience can be exactly what you need to thrive again. *Resilience* is a characteristic that permits a person to experience extreme hardships. It is the characteristic that enables a parent to get knocked down over and over again, rebounding each time with increased strength and fortitude. Letting these traumatizing experiences alter your course of life, your purpose for life, can deflate you emotionally, mentally, and spiritually, maybe to the point of losing your will to live. Your willingness to carry on in spite of adversity can bring you renewed strength and purpose if you are willing to lean into God, asking for health and mercy in your time of need.

When facing the devil's lies, you will need to develop resilience by nurturing your personal faith in God. In this process, you will need to also foster self-care, allowing your life to slow down, taking precautions to cut back on the most demanding activities in your life. This extra breathing room, so to speak, will allow you to spend more time in prayer, getting closer to the Lord, cultivating a deeper relationship. God can help you simplify your life to what's important in maintaining your mental, physical, and spiritual health. God will give you guidance for spiritual support from focusing on his Word, guiding you to the right support group or addiction counselor that will help you distinguish truth from lies.

> Therefore we do not lose heart. Though outwardly we are wasting away, yet inwardly we are being renewed day by day. For our light and momentary troubles are achieving for us an eternal glory that far outweighs them all. So we fix our eyes not on what is seen, but on what is unseen, since what is seen is temporary, but what is unseen is eternal. (2 Corinthians 4:16–18, NIV)

How can you help motivate your chemically dependent child?

Substance abuse and mental health services administration (SAMHSA) defines *motivation* as "internal and external forces and influences that move an individual to become willing and able to achieve certain goals and engage in the process of change."[32] Motivation is a key factor for anyone to make certain behavioral changes. It is fundamental in initiating change, as well making sustaining change.

Motivation for your addicted child to get clean and sober can come from both pain and hope. Pain acquired from the suffering of negative consequences brought about from chemical dependency can be a great motivator. Also, pain will occur as the euphoria from the drugs diminish. It's important for you to remember to not interfere with the negative consequences that will eventually ensue from bad choices they make while continuing in their addiction. Hope is also a great motivator. Every addict has a place in their heart where their hopes and dreams still exist. Hope is hard to diminish; and where there is hope, your child's dreams for a better life still exist, motivating them to reach their God-given potential.

Mike Speakman, founder of PAL and author of the *Four Seasons of Recovery* emphasizes the importance of how you, as a parent, can make some crucial changes in yourself that will make a difference in how you can motivate your addicted son or daughter.

> First, you must promise them you will accept their resistance to change, because now you understand that this a normal

attitude for someone who is chemically dependent (don't fight it). Secondly, you must learn how to shift your focus from helping and fixing their problems to allowing them to help themselves. Thirdly, you will need to set boundaries and consequences and learn to enforce them.[33]

Listen to my words... I, the LORD, reveal myself to them in visions, I speak to them in dreams. (Numbers 12:5, NIV)

What are you doing to promote change?

As a parent of an addicted child, you probably feel at times that you are traversing between sanity and insanity. Perhaps you are losing vital sleep because of the erratic and irresponsible behavior you are observing in your son or daughter's chemical dependency. Your desperation should provoke you to realize that you will need some professional guidance and support from groups like PAL and Al-Anon to help you extract vital information and knowledge. Moving forward in your purpose to help promote positive change in your son or daughter will require determination and tenacity.

Two persuasive things you can do to help promote change in your loved one is to acknowledge your child's positive behavior and set clear boundaries with consequences to prevent negative behavior. Reinforcing positive behavior helps create an environment and atmosphere of love and support. By choosing to respond to your child's positive behavior and actions, you are laying the important groundwork for them to continue to make constructive behavioral changes that will facilitate a sober life. Setting boundaries with clear consequences is the other strategy for helping to discourage negative behavior in your chemically addicted child. It's most effective when you use both of these methods together.

Another factor to help motivate your addicted child to change their behavior and attitude is to change the conversation to be more positive. They will be more optimistic when you are more optimistic. Being optimistic will give them a better chance for recovery. Let them know that they are not helpless, and their situation is not permanent. When you believe that this is true, your child will believe it too. Don't set your expectations for change too high. If we expect unhealthy behavior to change quickly and completely, we are likely to be disappointed.

> See, I am doing a new thing! Now it springs up; do you not perceive it? I am making a way in the desert and streams in the wasteland. (Isaiah 42:19, NIV)

Do you wonder if you will survive let alone thrive again?

As a parent of addicted child, you are probably having a difficult time picturing yourself surviving this horrific drama, let alone thriving again. Feeling the tension between grief and hope has perhaps caused your soul to dry up like a fallen autumn leaf, thrusting you into survival mode. There are many circumstances in life that can push you into survival mode, death of a loved one, a serious life-threatening illness, or a divorce that can produce a bitter and angry heart. The question is, can you rise above these difficult trials, especially with having an addicted child? Right now it may seem like an impossible dream to feel fully alive again with joy and peace in your life.

Dysfunction along with an evil dimension can reverse the course of your life, leaving your heart pulverized. You're worn out from the fight to save your loved one. When this happens, it's important to remember to slow down and set an even pace to rightly reconnect with God. Your soul is designed to refuel by allowing yourself to have some down time. Life is best lived at an even and sustainable pace. God has built into your soul a rhythm and pace that restores your soul. Cheat that pace and there will be consequences.

When you come to God, you get a healthy portion of grace. God's grace can bring you the right kind of faith that will lead to peace and rest. God is great, good, trustworthy, wise, able, and loving. God is interested in your growth through the storms. Having a chemically addicted child is one of the most difficult storms a parent can encounter. God wants you to set a sensible pace with your life, setting right priorities and dealing with a sensible amount of pressure. Letting go of self and humbling ourselves before God, believing He is as big as our pain and fear, will allow you to live outside of the shadow of addiction. Connect with God by praying, reading His Word, and meditating on his Word. God is in the middle of your battle. You can do all things through the power of God. You can thrive again. Decide what you want for yourself, thinking about your own dreams and not the dreams you had for your children. Try to release your kids to God, even to the worst-case scenario. Remember the Al-Anon slogan, "Let go and let God."

> Praise be to the God and Father of our Lord Jesus Christ, the Father of compassion and the God of all comfort. (2 Corinthians 1:3–4, NIV)

Do you want to let go of the chaos in your life?

As a parent of an adult son or daughter who is chemically addicted to alcohol, drugs or both, you can find yourself struggling to find peace and tranquility in your life. Maybe you find your child's life out of control, as well as your own. This was not part of what you bargained for when you became a parent. You might be far enough along in this chaotic journey that you now realize you can't fix their addiction issues. Remember the Al-Anon slogan, "You didn't *cause* it, you can't *control* it, and you can't *cure* it" (the three *C*'s).

There are some things that parents can do to help, support, and love their addicted child. Parents have the ability to be an important motivator, influencing change in their child in a positive way. You also have the power to be a negative influence by enabling their behavior with things like lecturing, paying a bill, giving them money for gas, etc. Building self-esteem comes from confronting and solving their own problems without Mom or Dad's help. When you use enabling behavior, you are sending a subliminal message to your addicted child that says they are not capable of solving their own problems.

As a parent wanting to continue to love and support your chemically addicted child, it is important to remember to say encouraging words. Mike Speakman, founder of PAL (parents of addicted loved ones), suggests using words like, "I believe in you. I'm praying for you. I know you are going to beat this problem; how can I help you help yourself; I hear-by resign as your rescuer." Another good one is "this is my home. It's not a detox center. It's not rehab. I'm not your counselor or a professional. I'm your mom/dad."[34]

Along with changing some of your language that you use with your son or daughter, it would be wise to start setting boundaries and consequences. To begin this process, start with baby steps, beginning with a boundary that would be uncomplicated to accomplish like telling them you will no longer pay for their cell phone (give a specific date); this is an adult responsibility. Your love one will probably be quite upset about this change, so be cautious not to get into an argument about it.

> But everything should be done in a fitting
> and orderly way. (1 Corinthians 14:40)

Is conflict a constant in your life?

Conflict can dominate a relationship when alcohol/ drugs are in the picture. There are many difficulties that can arise when you have a son or daughter who is caught in the throes of addiction. In the midst of these difficulties, it's not uncommon to buttheads. We see our addicted child make bad choices that will harm them, as well as others, so we step in to offer advice that may not be welcome. Conflict is a part of life; but when addiction is the main culprit in a conflict, how does it get resolved?

The answer is it may not. As long as your son or daughter is abusing alcohol/drugs, there will be conflict in your relationship. However, conflict can be managed. It's important to have a voice acknowledging your feelings, but be responsible for how you express your opinions. Anger is not the problem, but knowing how to direct your anger appropriately is called anger management.

It's important for you to release anger as soon as you can so that you don't build resentments that get more difficult to get rid of later. You may not voice your anger perfectly, and they may not be received well. Thomas Jefferson said, "When angry, count to ten before you speak; if very angry, a hundred."

Everyone has a point of view. It is important to remember that you may need many points of view in order to cope with the difficulties of having an addicted child. So when your child takes a different position from yours, you have a choice. You can assume that one of you is wrong and start defending yourself or try and understand where they are coming from, even though their outlook might be distorted because of their substance abuse. If the conflict is too difficult to solve, you can choose to rest your case and walk away, letting them know that you wish to continue the discussion at a later time, giving you both a reprieve to think about what each has said. It's all right to disagree, respecting each other's right to think differently. Voltaire said, "Think for yourself and let others enjoy the privilege of doing the same."

> My dear brothers, take note of this: Everyone should be quick to listen, slow to speak and slow to become angry, for man's anger does not bring about the righteousness life that God desires. (James 1:19–20, NIV)

Are you practicing self-care?

When you are knee-deep in the throes of one crisis after another, you have probably lost interest in yourself, focusing solely on your addicted son or daughter. Reducing your misery, by taking some action to take care of yourself, will help put some distance between you and the end of your rope. Making an effort to reduce your suffering is not only good for you but also good for your addicted child, allowing your relationship with your child to slightly relax. A chemically addicted child tends to be rebellious, think they know it all, and is very sensitive of you telling them who they are, creating serious tension in your relation-ship with them. The goal is to make choices that will help develop a healthy relationship with your son or daughter; one of those choices should be practicing self-care.

Think back to a time when your child was normal, not involved with alcohol/drugs. Did your routine change from that period to now? What were the things you use to do for yourself? Whether engaging in fun activities such as going to the movies or to making time for a haircut or massage, you need to involve yourself again with those things that made you feel good, that helped your confidence and self-esteem. Devoting time and energy to something good outside your fears and concerns for your son or daughter will help you build the strength and courage to tolerate what you as a parent can't change and that to which you can change.

Modeling healthy behavior can be an important role for you to undertake in order for you to gain patience and energy while dealing with issues and problems created by your chemically dependent child. When you start to engage in self-care, you will become a happier and calmer person able to contribute to making the mood more conducive to the change you hope to see in your child.

> Do you not know that your bodies are temples of the Holy Spirit, who is in you, whom you have received from God? You are not your own; you were bought at a price. Therefore honor God with your bodies. (1 Corinthians 6:19–20, NIV)

Are you feeling lost when trying to help your addicted child?

Feeling lost when you are trying to find answers to help your addicted son or daughter is normal because you are probably new to the addiction world. It can be painful, frustrating, and downright scary. The readily available supply of alcohol and drugs can be threatening to parents who know addiction can change their child for the worst. To see someone you love disappear before your eyes while standing right in front of you can send you out of control. Your emotions spiral up and down and get in the way of making sound decisions.

There is no set scientific formula for solving your child's substance use issue. There is only theory which can benefit you in your time of need. You need to sort through different approaches and find what's right for you. When you find the right fit, whether it be individual counseling, group support, or reading books on this subject, it should be something that you understand and can follow through on. In a PAL meeting, we often remind each other, "Remember it's not a sprint. It's a marathon." Gaining the knowledge and tools you will need is a process.

Learning to set boundaries is necessary, but many parents struggle with this parenting tool. If you find yourself saying one thing and then not following through with it, you can cause more damage than good. Also, allowing natural consequences to happen can be a struggle for parents. Many parents want to jump in at the first sign of trouble and fix the problem for their addicted child (helicopter parent). You must be clear with yourself first on what boundaries you can set and what you will keep. It's important that you don't send your child mixed messages because this will not promote the change you desire in your son or daughter.

This is a time when you can turn to God for help and direction through prayer. Turn to your pastor for guidance or a good addiction counselor for information on drugs and sources for help. Your child's welfare is too important to procrastinate. Drug and alcohol problems progressively get worse, so strike and nip this problem in the bud with a plan to move forward on gaining the knowledge and support you will need to fight for your child's sobriety.

> A man who remains stiff-necked after many rebukes will suddenly be destroyed— without remedy. (Proverbs 29:1)

Do you feel stuck?

Over the course of time, as a parent of an addicted son or daughter who is not getting sober or continues to relapse, you can feel stuck, not knowing where to turn. You have gotten discouraged and disheartened to the point where it is affecting your own well-being and sanity. Your life seems to be as unmanageable as your child's. Sometimes you feel that no matter what you do to try and help them, things continue to get worse, leaving you with an overwhelming fear for your own life, as well as your child's. When you think you have tried everything to help them turn their life around only to find failure once again, you have probably reached the end of your rope. You are not alone in this feeling. Most parents of an addicted child feel the same way, stuck.

The good news is that this feeling of being stuck can be a turning point if you take the necessary steps to change your own attitude and behaviors. As we say in the addiction world, "If nothing changes, nothing changes." If you haven't seen a therapist for yourself or been to a support group with parents going through the same challenges and issues, you better get yourself to one now. Every day you wait could be a day closer to getting unstuck. Hope can be right around the corner if you agree to make changes in yourself, finding proven methods that can help you and your child.

With the help of God, our creator, and others who have traveled the same path of addiction, you will find a reason to believe that there is hope regardless of your circumstances. You can begin to take steps to realizing the dreams for your child while maintaining their sobriety, as well as your own dreams that are free from worry and despair. God has a plan. Even if we can't understand it day-to-day, that plan includes better times ahead for you.

> My comfort in my suffering is this: Your
> promise preserves my life. (Psalm 119:50,
> NIV)

Are you helping or hindering your child's chances for success?

Having an addicted child dependent on alcohol or drugs is one of the most difficult positions you will find yourself in your lifetime. However, life is not about escaping from the pain and brokenness of this world. Instead, it's about being honest about your hurt and pain, walking with Jesus to bring healing, hope, and peace into your life, as well as others. God's plan can be mysterious, especially when you're in the midst of a difficult season. Keep in mind God can sometimes use painful experiences to prepare us for his greater plan.

As a parent of an addicted son or daughter, you can choose a course of action for success if you can keep an open mind to changes in yourself. This takes courage, courage to change. Mike Speakman tells parents, "One of the first changes that will have a positive effect on your child's progress toward sobriety is moving from a viewpoint of how can I help you to a perspective of 'How can I encourage you to help yourself.'"[35] This is a transformation in your thinking that will take time to alter. As a parent, you naturally feel responsible for the actions and behavior of your child, so you tend to try to fix, protect, rescue, and control your child's behavior. Instead, you could have a more positive effect on change if you show empathy, encourage, listen, and be sensitive to their desire to want change.

Fear and pain can trigger manipulative behaviors in yourself, which will only prolong the cycle of "how can I help you," rather than "how can I encourage you to help yourself?" Making this shift helps bring about change in your attitude for the larger topic of "enabling." As you make this shift in your thinking from fixing to helping, you will begin to realize what healthy helping looks like and what is unhealthy. Mike Speakman says in his book, *The Four Seasons of Recovery*, "Caretaking is how you raise a child; care-giving is how we help an adult. It may be difficult for you to make this shift in your thinking because your addicted child acts like a child therefore you feel you have to treat them like one. When you make this shift in how you help your addicted son or daughter, 'sometimes you have to believe in them more than they believe in themselves. The question becomes, 'Can you do this, if you knew it might save their life?'" The goal is to start becoming your adult child's role model and not consider yourself their life coach. A good question to ask yourself when deciding to "help" is whether you are doing it for their best interest or to make yourself feel better. [36]

> What we teach ourselves with our thoughts and attitudes is up to us. (In All Our Affairs)

> So, as those who have been chosen of God, holy and beloved, put on a heart of compassion, kindness, humility, gentleness, and patience. (Colossians 3:12, NIV)

Chapter 8

Acceptance
Gradual Recovery, Using
Truth to Move Forward

The Truth will set you Free. (John 8:32)

Are you open to seeking counsel?

A wise person understands that wisdom must be pursued, and the best source is always God's Word. Scripture is the plum line to which all other perspectives are compared and found to be truthful and right or false and wrong. God's Word teaches that no one is omniscient, so it is wise to consult trusted people. Outside counsel is used to arm a wise person with resources to navigate the difficult problems and complexities of life, such as addiction in your son or daughter.

The wise person seeks guidance from a variety of advisors. You should not hesitate to seek wisdom from many counselors. You really haven't heard or listened to another person until you can repeat back their view. The wisest course of action is often best gleaned from the strongest insights, cancelling out the weakest ones. This process allows God to direct plans to you in new creative ways.

Although too much advice or overanalysis can hinder the planning process, more advice is usually better than less. So after gathering plenty of advice and proceeding with a thoughtful course of action, a wise individual keeps seeking the confirmation of the Holy Spirit, experts in the field, and others who have had similar experiences. Addiction is a complex issue and cannot be solved by yourself. Be wise and seek counsel and then determine what to take away. A good Al-Anon slogan to remember is "Take what you want and leave the rest."

In contrast to seeking counsel, a fool withdraws from community of support. Therefore, he forfeits receiving the kind of affirmation and accountability that keeps his life on track. A fool does not seek advice because he wants to be left alone to pursue his own remedies, often in great haste. After accepting the truth about your addicted child, plan to reach out and find a good addiction counselor or a group support organization such as PAL (parents of addicted loved ones) or Al-Anon.

> Without counsel plans fail, but with many advisors they succeed. (Proverb 15:22, NIV)

Do you want to break out from the drama of addiction?

Drama is a symptom of addiction. Every parent of an addicted son or daughter is pulled into a life full of drama. The drama is constant and seems to never end, causing parents to lose sight of life's joys and simple moments of pleasure. Life keeps slipping by with no hope of feeling relief, comfort, and security in the knowledge of ever getting a normal life back again. Of course, you desire a life where you can feel joy and gratitude in a world full of possibilities and dreams.

As a parent of an addicted loved one, you must learn how to break free of the life of addiction filled with darkness and chaos. The first step you need to take is to come to the realization that you can't do the work of freeing your child from addiction. They must do the work themselves. Helping your kid grow into maturity is part of being a good parent; but when they become adults with addiction in the picture, it stagnates their ability to mature and grow emotionally. This is when parents with an addicted son or daughter can get caught up in the drama of addiction by adapting to their child's addicted behavior.

Your adult child needs to take responsibility for their dependence on alcohol or drug use, forcing them to face the pain and natural consequences stemming from their addictive behavior. Physical and emotional exhaustion from your child's addiction can often be your experience when you are caught in one of life's dilemmas that seems impossible to understand and deal with. You are unable to find the answers you need. Your natural emotional reaction is to feel hopeless.

Sometimes it's extremely difficult for parents to decide on what they think is best over the long run. A parent's first instinct is usually to try and fix the problem as quickly as possible. Drama can only be eliminated when you can detach and let go, letting your child experience the consequences of their bad choices, stepping out of the way and taking care of your own life and responsibilities. God reminds us that He is the one in control. He is at work in your child's life. Maybe God needs you to get out His way because you're not helping your child. You're actually impeding their recovery by trying to rescue. Again, you can remind yourself that you didn't cause the addiction. You can't control it, and you can't cure it.

> My flesh and my heart failed; but God is the strength of my heart. (Psalm 73:26, NIV)

Is it time to set boundaries with consequences?

As a parent of a chemically dependent son/daughter, you soon recognize that something must change in order to bring balance back into your life. Change is not always easy because you have fallen into behaviors and attitudes that fit into your comfort zone. Your adult addicted child has challenged your comfort zone impacting your life, especially your self-care. Maybe you have been trying to control the issues and problems caused by your addicted loved one, or maybe there is a deeper lesson in allowing manipulation to interfere with your well-being. When dealing with the drama caused by addiction, life may be pushing and hurting you to the point where change must happen. Boundaries are one of the important lessons to learn in this change process. If your son/daughter has pushed you to your limits, it is time for you to educate yourself on how to set boundaries and consequences.

Give yourself permission to allow boundaries and consequences to change your life and set you free from manipulation and the inability to say no. Much of the time, you have probably continued to parent your addicted kids after adulthood. Now that they are adults, your parenting style should change from that of control to that of releasing control and allowing them to make their own choices no matter how bad those choices may be, including the pain and suffering that may come from those choices. How else do you learn but by trial and error? Protecting, lecturing, arguing, or fixing is not the right reaction. Let go and let them become their own person. Slowly they will learn adult coping skills that will help them become independent and responsible adults.

When you realize you own your power to self-care, you begin to set boundaries to protect that self-care. In your new adult-to-adult relationship with your son/daughter, you can begin to set consequences for what happens when those boundaries are crossed. When your child oversteps those boundaries, they will learn to handle those consequences as adults. You may get some flack. That's to be expected, but you can't presume to control their reactions. Your adult child is bound to react when you do things differently in the process of nurturing yourself because it might negatively affect them. It's important to let them have their feelings and reactions, but you must continue to set boundaries that protect your well-being, learning to take a little resentment in the name of self-care. In Melody Beattie book, *Beyond Codependency,* she states, "We need to know how far we'll go, and how far we'll allow others to go with us. Once we understand this, we can go anywhere."[37] Here's an example of setting a boundary: "If you continue to abuse drugs/alcohol, you cannot live in our home. You will need to find your own place." It's up to you where you start with boundaries but take that first step to help move forward in the self-care process.

> Do you not know that your bodies are temples of the Holy Spirit, who is in you, whom you have received from God? You are not your own; you were bought at a price. Therefore honor God with your bodies. (1 Corinthians 6:19–20 NIV)

Are you seeking a deeper level of self-awareness?

Because your addicted son or daughter has chosen to use alcohol/drugs, are you unable to set your attention back on yourself and the needs of your other family members? As you begin a process of educating yourself on addiction, you will begin to realize where your responsibility truly lies, your child's or your own.

Through education on addiction and recovery, you will start recognizing the need for change in yourself, a transition. When you start focusing on changes in yourself, you may feel that you are neglecting your addicted child; but it in reality, you are not living your life totally for him or her. If they are legal age, they are free to make their own decisions which includes the freedom to fail or succeed.

For parents, this can be a time to change old habits, habits that are no longer useful. Before changing a habit, you must become aware of self which is called self-knowledge or self-awareness. This is not an easy goal and one that is usually avoided until a major event changes your outlook on life. A person usually will try to avoid change because it will require them to open up and share with another person, a family member, friend, counselor, coach, or pastor. This support person will help you see what is cleverly hidden in the unconscious part of your mind.

Changing old habits that are no longer useful can be difficult. The history that you have with your child that included many exchanges with routine responses to their unwanted behavior has not worked, so you need to be willing to change an old habit so that the outcome also changes. As the AA slogan points out, "If nothing changes, nothing changes." But like anything else that is worthwhile, changing habits takes time. The first step in the process of changing a habit is becoming aware of what that useless habit is. The second is practicing a new behavior/habit that you have chosen to replace the old one. It has been said that to replace an old habit with a new one, you must repeat it twenty-one times. This process forces you to pay attention to what you are doing and saying, as well as why. You will learn to recognize which habits that are working for you and those that are working against your best intentions. Get started; don't get distracted!

> "Can anyone hide in secret places so that
> I cannot see him?" declares the Lord. "Do
> not I fill heaven and earth?" declares the
> Lord. (Jeremiah 23:24, NIV)

Do you need encouragement?

Parents of an addicted son or daughter are often needing and searching for encouragement because their lives have become unmanageable. When you become negative and pessimistic, harmful stress hormones can inhibit your concentration, diminish your ability to think clearly, tending to create knee-jerk reactions rather than calm and rational thinking. Depending on how long you have been riding the roller coaster of addiction, you will get to a point where you run out of ideas on how to help your loved one. After accepting the truth about your child's addiction, this is the time when you could use some real encouragement.

Encouragement is essential to maintaining a positive attitude, especially when things are difficult and uncertain. When you are looking for encouragement, you usually need support, confidence, and hope, someone or something that can inspire, motivate, embolden, or uplift you. Encouragement can be far-reaching, often making a difference on whether you can weather a storm.

Encouragement for a parent of an addicted child can come from several sources. The most frequently endorsed in the addiction field are counselors, support groups, and pastors. These are sources that can give you the encouragement and suggestions you need to stay positive while your child is fighting addiction issues.

Encouragement is also needed for your addicted son or daughter. You may be the most influential person in your child's life, therefore in the best position to support, pray for, believe in, and journey with him or her. All the more reason for you to find the encouragement you need because they will need encouragement and support from you to find sobriety and keep it. There are times when loving someone means standing with him or her in the middle of major mistakes and shortcomings. We have all heard stories of a mother or father who will continue believing in, advocating for, and supporting their son or daughter through thick and thin with encouragement through unwavering patience and unconditional love. In order to be encouraging, we must find encouragement for ourselves.

> Be prepared in season and out of season; correct, rebuke and encourage—with great patience and careful instruction. (2 Timothy 4:2, NIV)

Is "acceptance" the answer to your problems?

Admitting you are powerless isn't a statement of despair and desperation but rather an acceptance statement of your limitations, leading you to lean on the Lord. Like other parents, you may be reluctant to admit that you have been dealt a hand of cards you have no idea how to play. A parent's natural impulse is to try and take control. At some point, you will realize that you need to yield all your concerns into the hands of your child's creator. Acceptance can produce the ability for you to let go, the hardest task of all.

Most parents find it difficult, if not impossible, to let go of their child. You might think that you are too nice, too weak, or too scared, feeling it would be cruel and unloving. It just doesn't feel like the right thing to do. On the contrary, the kind of detaching that is healthy and good is to separate yourself from the adverse effects of your child's destructive behaviors. You are not responsible for your child's problems or their recovery. Detaching allows you to let go of your obsession with your child's destructive behavior. You can start reaping emotional, psychological, and spiritual rewards by learning to detach.

The following statement was written anonymously, making it very clear why "acceptance" is so important to parents, as well as the alcoholic/addict:

> Acceptance is the answer to all my problems today. When I am disturbed, it is because I find some person, place, thing or situation—some fact of my life unacceptable to me. I can find no serenity until I accept that person, place thing or situa-

tion as being exactly the way it is supposed to be at the moment. Nothing, absolutely nothing, happens in God's world by mistake; unless I accept life completely on life's terms, I cannot be happy. I need to concentrate not so much on what needs to be changed in the world as on what needs to be changed in me and in my attitudes. (Anonymous Writer)

Is anything too difficult for the Lord? (Genesis 18:14, NIV)

Do you have the courage to change?

When I was first introduced to the Al-anon program, we read from one of the Al-Anon-approved daily devotional books *Courage to Change* at each meeting. I thought to myself, *Why would I need to change? It's my addicted child that needs to change.* Secondly, why would it take courage for me to change?

Desperation led me to my first Al-Anon meeting. I thought perhaps I could find answers on how to change my child. After all, they were the one with the addition issues. As I continued attending the weekly meetings, I realized that I needed recovery just like my child. Recovery for me meant I needed to make changes. My recovery meant it had to begin with me, not my child.

At first, the thought of change was daunting. The need to change my thinking, my belief system, and my view on addiction was overwhelming. Looking around the meeting room and seeing other parents following the program with success, I began to understand the concept of courage and the need for changes in myself. Perfectionism, procrastination, and paralysis were three of the worst effects of alcoholism on my life. I was determined that I could not move forward with my life if I did not start making the changes necessary for a life where I could experience joy and happiness again.

Realizing the need for change in myself meant I had to begin to remove the blocks that were getting in the way to joy and happiness. Because of the Al-Anon program, I began to look for fears, anger, hurt, and shame from my past. We all bury feelings that can affect our present life. Subconsciously we have buried beliefs about ourselves and others that can interfere with finding success in the quality of our relationships today. This process should be done with love and compassion for ourselves, extracting any guilt and exposing it for what it really is, self-criticism. Not useful if we want change!

Remember that problems and human limitations have benefits, keeping us from pride and giving God the opportunity to demonstrate his desire for us to become all that we can be.

> Therefore we do not lose heart. Though outwardly we are wasting away, yet inwardly we are being renewed day by day. For our light and momentary troubles are achieving for us an eternal glory that far outweighs them all. So we fix our eyes not on what is seen, but on what is unseen. For what is seen is temporary, but what is unseen is eternal. (2 Corinthians 4:16–18, NIV)

Do you understand how to detach with love?

There's a slogan in Al-Anon, "Let go and let God." In Al-Anon and PAL, you will learn that one of the most significant things that a parent can learn is how to let go. However, it is very difficult to let go when problematic situations cause worry and anxiety. For your adult child with addiction issues, it is time to practice giving up control along with learning how to set strong boundaries and consequences.

While you are learning about your own recovery, you will find it necessary to make changes. Therapists often use the AA slogan, "If nothing changes, nothing changes." Change can be difficult, especially when you are the type of person, like me, who thinks you can fix all of your child's problems by yourself. But after time, you learn that nothing you have done to help your addicted child has worked. Coming to the realization that something else might work, you can begin to open yourself up to understanding the importance of change and the significance of becoming willing to change.

In a support meeting, you will hear the Al-anon slogans "detach with love" and "let go and let God." They are reminders that there is nothing we can say or do to stop our addicted child's destructive behaviors. Detaching helps you let go of your fixation to control and resolve your child's addiction issues.

God is interested in your growth through the storms. Dealing with an addicted child is one of those storms. People and problems expose your heart; but with the proper motivation, you can come to God to get a healthy portion of His grace and mercy to strengthen and encourage you in the process of detaching. Believe that God loves your child no matter what mistakes they have made. He will reconcile them to himself, one way or another. As a parent, you must not interfere in this process and get between God and your child in the process of letting them suffer the natural consequences of their bad choices. Trusting in God is always the right choice, regardless of how things appear.

> We know that we all possess knowledge. Knowledge puffs up, but love builds up. The man who thinks he knows something does not yet know as he ought to know. (1 Corinthians 8:1–2, NIV)

Do you understand that "reinforcement" can be the driver of change?

Parents can take an active role in reinforcing the path that their chemically dependent child decides to take for positive change leading to sobriety. Reinforcement can be used with the many choices that can influence your child to choose a particular action, as well as the surrounding environment around them that supports or discourages that choice. Change is not easy, especially when fighting addiction. Changing the way you as a parent think about supporting change in your addicted child can be an important factor when trying to restore the relationship and encourage recovery.

You have probably tried to make some positive changes in your life and found it difficult to stick to your commitment. For example, maybe you have decided you need to lose some weight, so you decide to exercise regularly but then struggle to stick to the plan. Maybe each time you attempted to reach your weight goal and struggled to keep the weight off, it became more difficult to stay optimistic. This is why positive reinforcement is so import when making changes whether they're your changes or that of your child.

Change is difficult for everyone, particularly for those with addiction issues. It's a process for learning new ways to see yourself by changing your behaviors and making changes in your attitudes while moving out of your comfort zone. Change usually follows a zigzag course; so try to understand and remain positive, keeping your own balance, worrying less, and staying supportive. Mike Speakman says statements like the following can be very beneficial for your chemically dependent child: "I love you. I will always love you," "I can see the changes you are working on. Changes are hard. I'm proud of you," "I believe in you."[38]

When it comes to reinforcement, you will need to embrace specific strategies when dealing with your addicted child such as rewarding good behavior and discouraging bad behavior. The idea of reinforcing the positive will give your child a desire to do more positive changing in order for him/her to receive your praise. Everyone loves hearing praise. It brings about encouragement that is needed to maintain sobriety. Over time, as you practice the reinforcement strategy, it will become clear that change is good for you, as well as your child. Creating an atmosphere for reinforcement between you and your child, where the appeal of change is mutual, gives your loved one the opportunity to recognize better options for change. Rather than demanding change, you are inviting change. Ask yourself: are you giving your child positive feedback for positive behavior?

> A good man brings good things out of the good stored up in his heart, and an evil man brings evil things out of the evil stored up in his heart. For the mouth speaks what the heart is full of. (Luke 6:45, NIV)

Have you been taught the Serenity Prayer and its meaning?

This powerful prayer reads, "Please grant us the serenity to accept the things we cannot change, the courage to change the things we can, and the wisdom to know the difference."

When I first started going to Al-Anon, we always started and ended the meeting with the Serenity Prayer. I began to understand that using this prayer is a useful and valuable tool. By repeating the prayer often, you begin to understand its simple but valuable meaning.

Serenity is what we seek from the cold cruel world of addiction. At times, we feel we are losing our sanity by trying to fix our adult child's addiction issues. After realizing that there is nothing we can do to fix their addiction, we desperately seek out answers to find our own sanity again. When insanity dominates our life, it robs us from realizing joy, comfort, and serenity. By learning to accept life as it is, you can bring about serenity for yourself.

"Courage to change" comes about when you realize that the only thing you have the power to change is your own character defects. Forget about half measures to change because, in reality, it only paralyzes you from making meaningful steps forward in your own spiritual journey. By taking action to make a change, you gain courage, asking God for the help and the courage to change. "The essence of all growth is a willingness to make a change for the better and then an unremitting willingness to shoulder whatever responsibility this entails."[39]

"Wisdom to know the difference" is when God has given us the ability to distinguish the things we can change from the things we cannot change. In other words, some things must be turned over to God. Then there are those times and situations where the wisest thing to do is nothing at all. Sometimes it's better to do nothing than to do something that makes the situation worse. Problems come when we make quick decisions or react to certain situations before thinking and praying about it.

Darkness and lack of spiritual understanding is the natural condition of our humanity. Paul makes it very clear that God has "made foolish the wisdom of this world" (1 Corinthians 1:20). Rather, "the foolishness of God is wiser than men" (1 Corinthians 1:25). "Cease from thy own wisdom!" (Proverbs 23:4).

Does your communication style include criticism and lecturing?

As parents of an addicted son or daughter, we often hear ourselves say, "Things have got to change, or I'll go out of mind with worry and fear?" It's true that many things need to change; but the only thing I can change, as a parent, is myself. This is difficult for parents to understand because we aren't the ones with addiction issues. The way a parent sees it is that their child needs to make the changes by getting into a recovery program and staying sober. In reality, this may be true; but as parents of an addicted child, this theory of change for us has been said to have big effects with regard for positive changes in our children.

Most often we react to their behavior with anger, criticism, accusations, and ridicule, which only adds to the drama. Parents can get caught up in the emotion of the moment reacting to their child rather than having a measured response. Remember this theory, "As I change my response toward my loved one, I also will be changing our relationship."[40]

The changes you make by giving a thoughtful response rather than a spontaneous reaction can make a big difference in your child's recovery. First, remember that sometimes silence is the best response. Second, you will need to avoid manipulating and controlling. Third, resist engaging in arguments and walk away if necessary. Forth, respond after thinking, praying, breathing or seeking counsel and advice. When you learn to respond rather than react, you are choosing to support rather than attack. Support consists of empathy, reassurance, respect, and encouragement.

Criticism and lecturing come from over-reacting rather than stopping and thinking about how you will respond. A helpful response takes time and thought.

> A man of knowledge uses words with restraint, and a man of understanding is even-tempered. Even a fool is thought wise if he keeps silent, and discerning if he hold his tongue. (Proverbs 17:27–28)

Is confusion distracting you from being content?

Does your son or daughter's addiction to alcohol or drugs get confusing at times, causing you to want to run away from life, leaving behind your world full of chaos and drama that you didn't cause or ask for? As a parent, you have always done your best, trying to find the best solutions available for your child when they have had difficult times and needed your support. But now that they have become an adult addicted to drugs/alcohol, you are realizing that things need to change as it relates to how you support and love them.

Has it ever occurred to you that perhaps you don't have to act and find solutions for your addicted child? In fact, because they are now adults, the responsibility for their own life now rests on them. Adulthood entitles them the freedom to make their own decisions and choices, whatever that may be and whatever may come from those decisions and choices. One of the hardest problems for you to face comes from watching your addicted child make poor decisions that are reflective of their unfortunate choice to abuse drugs/alcohol. Confusion for you can be the result of taking on responsibility that should be your child's, causing a wage of war within your mind. Doubts on what your next step should be in reaction to your son or daughter's substance abuse adds to the confusion.

When confusion, mayhem, uncertainty, or turmoil try to dominate your life, you can learn to turn to God for whatever you may be facing remembering the things you are grateful for. Contentment is a state of mind that you can help bring about by understanding and believing that God is in charge and has a plan and purpose for your child that will someday become a reality. Helen Keller wrote, "Everything has its wonders, even darkness and silence, and I learn, whatever state I may be in, therein to be content."

> I have learned to be content whatever the circumstances… I have learned the secret of being content in any and every situation… I can do everything through him who gives me strength. (Philippians 4:11–13, NIV)

What does letting go look like?

In the book *The Grace Awakening*, Charles Swindoll wrote:

"To let go does not mean to stop caring,
　　It means I can't do it for someone else.
To let go is not to cut myself off,
　　It's the realization that I can't control another.

To let go is not to enable,
>   but to allow learning from natural consequences.
To let go is to admit powerlessness,
>   Which means the outcome is not in my hands.
To let go is not to try to change or blame another,
>   I can only change myself.
To let go is not to care for,
>   but to care about.
To let go is not to fix,
>   but to be supportive.
To let go is not to judge,
>   but to allow another human being.
To let go is not to be in the middle arranging all the outcomes,
>   but to allow others to affect their own outcomes.
To let go is not to be protective;
>   It is to permit another to face reality.
To let go is not to deny,
>   but to accept.
To let go is not to nag, scold, or argue,
>   but to search out my own shortcomings and to correct them.
To let go is not to adjust everything to my desires,
>   but to take each day as it comes.
To let go is not to criticize and regulate anyone,
>   but to try to become what dream I can be.

To let go is not to regret the past,

but to grow and to live for the future.

To let go is to fear less and love more!"[41]

Do you understand that relationships can influence sobriety?

Relationships in your addicted child's life may influence relapse and healthy recovery more than any other areas of their life. In the first phase of recovery, the addicted person will primarily focus on themselves. Relationship work is usually the second stage in the process. Learning what healthy relationships look like and how to have a healthy relationship is one of life's crucial lessons.

Relationships involve many aspects of life including family, friends, God, business, nature, and self. When your child participates in life's journey, connecting to these relationships, it will influence their attitudes and emotions. It is noted in addition therapy that healthy relationships help build a strong recovery. So the strength and quality of the addicted person's relationships can be directly proportional to the strength and quality of their sobriety.

When your child is actively using, they are in relationship with their drug of choice, negatively affecting other relationships. When this occurs, other relationships have taken a back seat to the primary relationship of substance abuse. In the process of gaining their sobriety back, your child will need to learn to change the way they relate to family, friends, and acquaintances. Your child will need to feel support and safety from you during this process. Relating well with family again will take practice, requiring honesty, trust, and vulnerability from both parties.

As a parent, you are probably looking at your relationship solely in terms of your loved one's substance problem. However, there are areas in the relationship that work and other areas that are not working at all. Honesty is the best policy when it comes to relating to another person. A parent can begin by setting boundaries about your intended level of participation. You can talk about what your child can reasonably expect from you, because that is what you want to give. How your child deals with that is their issue. Parents have a right to ask and receive clear answers. You, as a parent, have a right to your own definitions and your own expectations. The boundaries and definitions of your relationship with your child will empower them and you to take care of that relationship. The clearer you can become with defining your relationship with your child, the more self-care you give yourself. You cannot force your child into a relationship with you or at a level you desire if your son or daughter does not want to. Each person has a choice in how invested they choose to be. Parent-sober-child relationships take a while to restore; but at some point, you should be able to define what that relationship looks and feels like as well as what the boundaries are.

> Above all, love each other deeply, because love covers over a multitude of sins. (1 Peter 4:8, NIV)

Do you understand the power of powerlessness?

As a parent of a chemically addicted child, you are probably experiencing an awareness of having no control. The feeling of powerlessness can overwhelm you, making it tough to carry on an active life filled with joy and contentment. The feeling of powerlessness will challenge you to turn to those that can help, parents that understand and can empathize with your situation. Their experiences can help you form a plan on how you will confront and move through this difficult time. Consider support groups such as Al-Anon, PAL (parents of addicted loved ones), Celebrate Recovery, and research their websites.

The twelve steps practiced in Al-Anon, AA, and NA (Nar-Anon) are critical for the person suffering from chemical dependency but also beneficial for parents suffering from codependency. The first step calls for accepting and admitting powerlessness over compulsions such as enabling. A parent can be both powerful and powerless at the same time. As a parent in pain, having a child with addiction issues, you will come to the realization that power and powerlessness come with the territory. As a parent, you have the power to make changes in yourself that will help your child make behavioral changes in themselves but also are powerless to make your addicted child change. Getting educated on addiction is a smart and powerful approach for helping your child.

Recognizing your powerlessness is the first step to empowering yourself. Surrender your mind and energy by letting go of your own willpower to change and control others. Stop trying to do what is impossible and give your energy over to doing what is possible, the ability to change your own attitudes and behaviors. Our life becomes unmanageable when we are focused on changing and controlling others. It's time to focus on your own recovery. It is a process, as well as a journey, a marathon, not a sprint.

> That God will grant them repentance leading them to the knowledge of the truth, and that they will come to their senses and escape from the trap of the devil, who has taken them captive to do his will. (2 Timothy 2:25–26, NIV)

Do you have an attitude of gratitude?

As a parent of an adult child who has a chemical addiction, you have probably gone through hell at times and wondered if you would survive the devastating effects it has had on you and your child. Maybe you even felt at times you were going insane, never being able to fully accept the reality of having an addicted child, along with all the problems that come along with addiction. Every day can bring challenges, heartache, and hopeless feelings.

When you face addiction, you may feel overwhelmed, unable to see the lessons that can come from this experience. One simple theory may help you see the lessons that can be absorbed through the difficult process of having an addicted child. Believe it or not, you can learn to say thank you to our heavenly Father for these difficult lessons which will assist you in your spiritual growth and expand your capabilities and understanding of the ups and downs of life's journey.

Rather than focusing on the problem, prayer should be our response to crisis. Our prayers should always begin with adoration and gratitude for the love that God has shown us through the sacrifice of his only begotten Son on the cross, never forgetting that God is holy and sovereign. Remember the story of Hannah who was in deep anguish because she could not have a child and was being ridiculed by other women. She went to the temple to pray, crying and admonishing the Lord to help her. Her prayers started with gratitude for God's never-ending love. Because of her humbleness and gratitude toward God, he heard her prayer and rewarded her with a son.

God is always working where you cannot see. Your part is to never lose heart, persevere, and do the best you can, leaving the results in His hands. Prayer was never meant to be a method for you to get things from God but rather our way of getting closer to God, to get more of God. In our desperation, we can get things turned around and lose our connection. Force gratitude; it can be the key that unlocks positive energy into your life and helps you from trying to manipulate life's outcomes.

> We were under great pressure, far beyond our ability to endure, so that we despaired even of life. Indeed, in our hearts we felt the sentence of death. But this happened that we may might not rely on ourselves but on God, who raises the dead. (2 Corinthians 1:8–9, NIV)

Are you ready to forgive?

Whether you realize it or not, eventually your child needs to be forgiven for the bad choices they have made which may be taking away your mental and physical well-being. Your pain, brokenness, anguish, financial strain, including sleepless nights are the worst depravity a parent can experience. You may be thinking that the only way you might forgive your child is for them to repent first. Even then, perhaps you might need to think about it first. Is forgiveness conditional or unconditional? Jesus taught us that forgiveness should be unconditional, taking a more freeing approach, teaching that forgiveness is a gift of grace.

Paul writes in Romans 5:7–11 how God demonstrates his own love for us in forgiveness:

> While we were still sinners, Christ died for us. Since now we have been justified by his blood, how much more shall we be saved from God's wrath through him! For if, when we were God's enemies, we were reconciled to him through the death of his Son, how much more, having been reconciled, shall we be saved through his life!

Another enormous example of forgiveness is Jesus Christ when, on the cross, He said, "Father forgive these people because they know not what they are doing." There was no repentance from the people who sentenced and killed Him. Christ's forgiveness did not condone or excuse the behavior. His forgiveness released them to God to deal with them.

As a parent with a wounded heart and painful memories, you can find healing and hope from Christ's example of forgiveness. However, recognize how your addicted child hurt you. It really doesn't matter if they meant to or not. You can hold your child accountable and not excuse their behavior; but at the same time, you are responsible for forgiving them. As a parent of an addicted child, forgiveness is a part of the process of getting back your life. M. Scott Peck wrote, "If we hold on to our anger, we stop growing and our souls begin to shrivel."[42] Again, use the Al-Anon slogan, "let go and let God."

> Bear with each other and forgive one another if any of you has a grievance against someone. Forgive as the Lord forgave you. (Colossians 3:13, NIV)

Chapter 9

A Personal Spiritual Journey Applying Truth Using Rigorous Honesty

Al-Anon and AA Twelve Steps

The twelve-step program

In Al-Anon and PAL, we can find the help and support we need to help us with addiction issues in our family, whether it be a child, a spouse, or sibling. In Al-non, we learn about how the twelve steps work which are the core beliefs of AA and the Al-Anon program. As a parent of an addicted child regularly attending the meetings, I agreed to work the twelve-step program. I was told that it would be a spiritual journey that would make a positive impact on my life. It would be challenging but would prove to be just what I needed to get my own life back in order, experiencing joy and peace that I so desperately needed and yearned for.

It didn't take many meetings for me to realize that I needed to make some changes in my thinking and attitude about addiction, as well as how I reacted to its issues and challenges. Realizing I did need to change, it became more and more apparent that it would take courage to make those changes.

Change can cause fear, making it difficult for us to want to change. It's always easier to do things the way we have always done things, remaining in our comfort zone rather than stepping out and trying something new and different. Our attitudes and behaviors have been a part of us for a long time. Like myself, you may be realizing that these attitudes and behaviors might need to be tweaked or modified to handle the difficult challenges that have resulted from having a child with an alcohol or drug addiction.

If we are not moving in a positive direction, perhaps we need to make some changes. We can do nothing to change the past; however, we don't need to keep making the same mistakes that are preventing positive change for the future. No one can make us change. No one can stop us from changing. No one knows the path for change. Bear in mind that it only takes a small change in our thinking for the process of change to begin. "The journey of a thousand miles begins with a single step," a quote from Lao Tzu. Sometimes the greatest changes and growth come out of painful times. It's the pain that motivates us to change, but it also your response to the pain that causes you to grow. Your attitude about the pain can change. A new and different response allowed me to gain spiritual blessings from the pain I was experiencing because I was willing to take the first step toward change. I hope by summarizing the need and benefits of the Al-anon steps, it will give insight into the importance of these steps and why they are used in most treatment approaches for parents, as well as an addicted child. This twelve step summary is the result of using various Al-Anon materials as well as opinions from other co-dependents that have worked through the twelve steps.

> Be comforted in the scripture, "For it is God who works in you to will and to do His good pleasure." (Philippians 2:13, NIV)

Are you ready to declare step 1?

In the first step, "We admitted we were powerless over addiction [enabling for parents]—that our lives had become unmanageable."

What does admitting to our powerlessness look like? Does it mean admitting that we are overwhelmed, overcome, or defeated? Admitting any of these issues is something we are not usually comfortable with. It goes against what we want to believe about ourselves. In the realm of addiction, we may find that no matter how hard we attempt to fix our circumstances or other people, we have been powerless in those attempts. We need to come to realize and admit our powerlessness over those that use drugs and alcohol so that we can deal with our pain and confusion that can consume our own lives. We have been powerless to change our situation or our child's addiction. To surrender means that I alone cannot defeat this disease. I need something else to help me, to humble myself and admit defeat, no longer struggling to regain control.

The disease has three conclusions: continued drug use, sobriety, or death. This disease progresses to the brink of being out of one's control, bringing along the severity of consequences and losses. As you have probably experienced, parents of addicted children want to take things into their own hands because we think we know what's best. Our efforts to control the disease/child rarely are successful.

Eventually we realize we are completely hopeless and lost. If we make the decision to call out for God's mercy and help, we usually are amazed at His grace and swiftness to action. However, God doesn't always help us in the way we have in mind, and we once again are tempted to rely on our own will instead of completely trusting in Him.

> No matter which way I turn, I can't make myself do right. I want to but I can't. When I want to do well I don't. And when I try not to do wrong, I do it anyway. (Romans 7:18–19)

Are you ready to affirm step 2?

"We came to believe that a power greater than ourselves could restore us to sanity." This is where parents of an addicted child can find hope. Although Christians don't struggle with the idea that God is the creator of earth and everything in it, our concept of God can be vague and unclear. We believe in God but may struggle with making God our true source of hope and the center of everything in our life. Every one forms their own concept of God through joyful times along with unfortunate circumstances that come along in everyone's life. Many people's view of God may have been distorted by childhood experience with our parents or maybe inaccurate or misleading messages from the pulpit. Perhaps we may be holding onto resentments because we believe God treated us unfairly or didn't come through for us when we needed His help, allowing bad things to happen to us. In step 2, we rethink our personal concept of God.

With many negative experiences that have skewed our perception of God, it is only natural that we would come to rely on our own self to manage our lives, as well as attempt to manage our addicted child's life. It is very difficult to stop relying on our own logic and rational and ask for help. In this step 2, we start to open up our mind, realizing we don't have all the answers. When we open our minds to a different way of thinking about God, we are showing the valuable quality of humility, helping us become more teachable.

God is calling us to look to Him, resting in the reality that He knows what He is doing. He *is* wisdom. He *is* truth. He *is* the sovereign Lord over all our circumstances, and His will shall be done (Ephesians 1:11), God often *drives* us to just give up our attempts to figure things out in our lives.

In Romans 7:18–19 (NIV), the psalmist understood the Lord's ways, writing these words:

> I love the Lord, for He heard my voice; He heard my cry for mercy. Because he turned his ear to me, I will call on him as long as I live.

Are you ready to perform step 3?

"We made a decision to turn our will and our lives over to the care of God as we understood Him." In step 3, we put our belief in a higher power into action, making a conscious decision to turn our will and our lives over to the care of the God, along with our willingness to allow God to work in our lives. At first, we may be willing only to a certain degree; but with time, we eventually learn to trust a power greater than ourselves.

Moving away from our self-will is required in this step. Keep in mind that self-will is made up of characteristics such as closed-mindedness, unwillingness, self-centeredness, and defiance. These characteristics, along with insanity, have made our lives unmanageable, keeping us in a continuous cycle of fear and pain. Insanity is sometimes defined as doing the same thing over and over again, expecting a different result. As parents we wear ourselves out in fruitless attempts to control everyone, including our addicted child, looking for ways we could force things to go as we wanted.

If you were like me, you may hesitate because you fear that you won't be happy with what your life will be like. Even though we do not know specifically how our life will be affected, we trust their will be progress in our growth despite our fears and uncertainty. God will take care of our lives better than we can when we make a commitment to our own emotional, physical, and spiritual welfare. When we take this step, we are taking a serious step to live our life differently than we have in the past.

Turning our will and our lives over to a higher power/ God, we let go of our self-centered will, providing a solution to the problems created by self-centeredness, resentments, manipulation, and control. Paul writes in Philippines 2:13, "For it is God who works in you to will and to do His good pleasure." He is *effectively energizing us* to accomplish His will, revealing a truth that can set us free in our daily walk. He alone is the energizer who will accomplish His good pleasure in us.

Are you ready to execute step 4 and 5?

Step 4: "Made a searching and fearless moral inventory of ourselves."

Step 5: "Admitted to God, to ourselves and to another human being the exact nature of our wrongs."

As parents, we ask ourselves if it is important to take action and work the steps just as our children are asked to do when they firmly commit to the AA program. For me, the answer was yes, becoming one of the most wonderfully fulfilling and important personal journeys I have ever taken. I thank God that I moved forward and did exactly as they asked me to do when I joined Al-Anon. Now I believe that every Christian would benefit immensely from this process. By doing this, we are in keeping with strengthening our faith for God's purpose for our life. Godly wisdom can come through these actions.

The fourth step is probably the hardest of all the steps because we are asked to make a list of all our defects of character, remembering all those we have hurt and offended along with any resentments that have manifested during our lifetime. We search out the flaws in our character, those things that can get in the way of personal success. We list people, organizations, customs, traditions, and rituals that have made us angry or caused resentments. While doing this, we ask ourselves why we were angry. Was it because it hurt our self-esteem, our finances, ambitions, our personal relationships, or we were hurt or threatened? After making this list, AA/Al-Anon requires us to admit our faults to ourselves, God, and another person. The purpose of this is somewhat like a Catholic confession. Have you heard the saying "we are only as sick as our deepest secrets?" Secrets can be released and never dealt with or spoken of again if we ask God to forgive. A life that includes resentments can lead to unhappiness. By doing this step, we are allowing ourselves to move from the past, only living in the present while looking forward to the future.

> And the God of all grace, who called you to eternal glory in Christ, after you have suffered a little while, will himself restore you and make you strong, firm and steadfast (NIV). (1 Peter 5:10, NIV)

Are you ready to perform step 6 and 7?

Step 6: "Were entirely ready to have God remove all these defects of character"

Step 7: "Humbly asked Him to remove our shortcomings"

In these steps, we ask God to give us the motivation and a willingness to let go of all our defects of character, not allowing anything to get in the way of ridding ourselves of all resentments. Otherwise, if we cling to anything, good or bad, it will get in the way of allowing God access to our innermost being. This means getting free of everything that might get in the way of our usefulness to God and others. God wants all of us, not just what we want him to have. We need to throw our pride out the door, bringing light to every dark corner of our life, withholding nothing. Once we have taken these steps, we will feel a sense of peace and serenity that we have never felt before. This is the essence of these two steps, allowing us to become closer to our Creator.

In recognizing how our egos got in the way of truth, playing God and creating our own false reality, we begin to humble ourselves, allowing God to direct and guide us in our daily situations. God has created us for a purpose, his purpose. Each of us has God-given talents and skills to help us in fulfilling God's purpose for our life.

In times of great sorrow, experiencing great pain and suffering, have you turned away from God? It's hard to make sense of great sorrow. Some tragedies can be so great no one simply gets over them or moves on. Actually, unexplainable sorrow is a great reason to turn toward God. He is our Savior who can transform our sorrow into joy and turn our lives from darkness toward the light. We begin this process by admitting we are in the darkness, looking for the light of truth, and then acknowledging our shortcomings so that we can move forward in our personal journey, seeking God's purpose for our life.

God is omniscient, all knowing, with knowledge of everything that has happened, is happening and ever will happen.

> God the Savior, who wants all men to be saved and to come to a knowledge of the truth. (Timothy 2:4, NIV)

Are you ready to move through step 8 and 9?

Step 8: "Made a list of all persons we had harmed, and became willing to make amends to them all."

Step 9: "Made direct amends to such people wherever possible, except when to do so would injure them or others."

After subjecting ourselves to self-appraisal, we need to keep moving forward and try to repair all the damage we have done, sometimes not knowingly, but the damage is still there. We have tried to live on self-will and running the show ourselves. Now, with the help of God, we have created a list of all persons we have harmed and are willing to make amends/apologies. Remember, at the beginning of our steps, we agreed that we would go to any lengths for victory over alcohol/drugs (for parents, our enabling and codependent behavior). We are merely trying to put our lives in order, realizing that we too may have had a part in our children's addiction issues.

When given the opportunity to listen to our apology, most people will recognize when we are trying to set right a wrong. Our fearless inventory will not only point our defects of character, our weakness, our need to compensate and please but also our need to try and make it right. Our unjustified actions, behavior, and hurtful words only further reveal our human fallacies and need for a higher power to help us remove our shortcomings. Removing these shortcomings will help us advance on life's journey with a clean slate.

When we approach the person whom we have decided needs our apology, under no circumstance should we criticize or argue. Simply we tell them that we will never get over our codependency until we have straightened out the past. We need to take care of our part of making things right, knowing that nothing is worthwhile will be accomplished until we do. Also, we should never tell the other person what he or she should do, never discussing what we think are their faults. If we stick to this plan with honesty and calmness, we will be grateful that we accomplished this task.

Good and upright is the Lord; therefore
he instructs sinners in his ways. He guides

the humble in what is right and teaches them his way. (Psalm 25:9, NIV)

Are you ready to act upon step 10?

Step 10: "Continued to take personal inventory and when we were wrong promptly admitted it."

Humility is the key component in accomplishing step 10, as well as completing the other steps. The steps become a means for us to change and to conform into Christlike human beings. This sanctification process is a slow process, as well as a painful process. Remember that anything worth changing for the good is worth the pain and anguish that may come with it. The old adage "no pain, no gain" rings true. Because of your willingness to build a relationship with our Creator by means of completing the twelve steps, it will not only teach you humility but will reward you with more of God's grace, increasing peace and power in your life.

Some parents might feel that this step is demeaning and unbecoming. In actuality, humility can be dignifying because it is characteristic that God calls his believers to possess, giving way to arrogance and pride. Humility is an honest and realistic view of ourselves in relationship to God and our fellow human beings. We all need to be rescued from ourselves. King David needed to be rescued from himself, and that process took God approximately ten years; don't become impatient with God in this sanctification process. He knows what he is doing. He is a sovereign God, omniscient (all knowing), omnipresent (fully present everywhere), and omnipotent (all powerful).

Problems and people expose your heart, giving you good reason to desire change in yourself. Becoming and behaving like a Christian is not difficult but rather impossible, but our Lord has done the work for us to be reconciled to God. We acknowledge that we can't but God can. God is sovereign over all our problems. Trust in God is always the choice, regardless of how things appear. Faith is living your life without scheming but rather placing God in the middle of everything you do and desire. In step 10, we acknowledge our mistakes right away and make amends where called for. With this step, we begin to see God's grace in our lives, moving beyond tolerance toward true love for family and friends.

> Humble yourselves, therefore, under God's mighty hand, that he may lift you up in due time. (1 Peter 5:6–7, NIV)

Are you willing and ready to take step 11?

"Sought through prayer and meditation to improve our conscious contact with God, praying only for knowledge of His will for us, and the power to carry that out."

As you move through the steps, your knowledge of God's grace grows, giving you an increased desire for a closer and more personalized relationship with Him. Through meditation and prayer, you can quiet the noise inside your head and that which comes from the world around you. When you allow this process to happen daily in your life, you will begin to hear his voice rather than your self-will disguised as God's still voice.

Maybe in the past, you scarcely knew what was good for you, so you found it inappropriate to ask God for knowledge and a better understanding of His will for you. Maybe the guilt and shame of your own sinfulness disheartened you. Whatever the case may be, God does not treat you the way your sins and mine deserve but rather treats all who seek knowledge of His will for us and all who believe, like His perfect Son. He gives His Word and His spirit to lead and guide us in a lifelong battle with sin. Returning to God for grace to repent is a mark of belonging to God. Although many times sin seems to win, God's promises and warnings can strengthen you. God credits Jesus's sinless life and death for sin to all who believe, giving you a new desire and ability to fight sin.

Be careful that anger does not take root when your pride is injured. It's easy for you to magnify the wrongs you might suffer, so your words can become weapons of revenge if you're not careful to pray for grace and strength to forgive. Your failure to forgive points out that you do not trust God's justice. Remember that revenge belongs to God alone. Pray for humility to use God's grace as a platform to share God's grace with others. Struggles and defeats and successes are God's training ground, a normal part of the sanctification process. God's firm grip can assure even the weakest believer eternal safety and joy.

> Let the wise listen and add to their learning, and let the discerning get guidance. (Proverbs 1:5, NIV)

Are your ready to carry out step 12?

"Having had a spiritual awakening as the result of these steps, we tried to carry this message to alcoholics (codependents), and to practice these principles in all our affairs."

The message is one of hope, love, comfort, and health, a way of living our lives that works. In meetings, we might hear, "Keep coming back. It works if you work it, and you're worth it."

The steps will never cease to exist in our lives. There are always times in our lives when we feel anger, despair, confusion, and disappointment. When we feel overwhelmed and desperate, we need to remember that the steps are always there for us. We believe that whatever we may be facing, we know that by working the steps, it will help.

We can carry the message of hope by modeling a better way of life. We understand that by showing others a better way of living, we can spread the message that the steps work. By doing our own recovery work, we become an example to others, demonstrating that there is hope. By living his message quietly rather than by boasting or lecturing, we convey a message that becomes powerful to those who are watching and listening.

By allowing our higher power to guide our attitudes and behaviors, we convey a strong message that the steps work. By leading by example, we can be more effective than trying to coerce someone into their own recovery. Trying to control others and caretaking are behaviors of codependency and not effective ways to convince someone that they need to change. We learn that the best way to help others is to demonstrate how we are taking care of ourselves, letting go of our need to help and control others.

> Praise be to the God and Father of our Lord Jesus Christ, the Father of compassion and the God of all comfort, who comforts us in all our trouble, so that we can comfort those in any trouble with the

comfort we ourselves have received from
God. (2 Corinthians 1:3–4)

The Bible defines comfort as to encourage, help, and
strengthen.

Notes

1   Internet anonymous entry: "I Hope You Never."

2   William Coleman, *Parents with Broken Hearts* (BMH Books, May 1, 2007).

3   William Cowper (n. d.), QuotesWave.com, accessed May 5, 2019, http://www.quoteswave.com/text-quotes/14687

4   Michael Speakman, *Four Season of Recovery for Parents of Alcoholics and Addicts* (Phoenix, Arizona: Rite of Press, 2014), 65.

5   "Types of Dysfunctional Families," Realistic Recovery, July 23, 2009.

6   Speakman, *Four Season*, 11.

7   Stanley J Grenz, David Guretzki, and Cherith Fee Nordling, *Pocket Dictionary Theological Terms* (InterVarsity Press: Downers Grove, Illinois, 1999).

8   Timothy Beals, Devotional, drawn from the NIV Hope in the Mourning Bible, Zondervan, 2013.

9   Substance Abuse and Mental Health Services Administration. Children living with substance-abusing or substance-dependent parents (National Household Survey on Drug Abuse) Office of Applied Studies, Rockville, Maryland, 2003, accessed www.oas.samhsa.gov/2k3/children/children.htm.

10 Speakman, *Four Season*, 71.

11 Ibid., 91.

[12] Ibid., 51.

[13] PAL (parents of addicted loved ones) Lesson #3, "Helping: Unhealthy vs. Healthy," June 2017.

[14] Speakman, *Four Season*, 43.

[15] Ibid., 25.

[16] Ibid., 46–47.

[17] Ibid., 47.

[18] Ibid., 79.

[19] Ibid., 48.

[20] Ibid., 58.

[21] PhD. Fred Chay, Inspired by *Friday with Fred* article.

[22] Speakman, *Four Season*, 58

[23] Center for Substance Abuse Treatment and Family Therapy. Treatment Improvement Protocol (TIP) Series, No. 39. HHS Publication No. (SMA) 15-4219. Rockville, Maryland: Substance Abuse and Mental Health Services Administration, 2004.

[24] Elizabeth Hartney, PhD, "Why Post-Acute Withdrawal can be a Barrier to Recovery," June 19, 2009.

[25] Speakman, *Four Season*, 68.

[26] Ibid., 194.

[27] https://addictionsandrecovery.org/is-addiction-a-disease.htm

[28] Kevin McCauley, Pleasures Unwoven, a personal journey about addiction, The Institute for Addiction Study, 2009.

[29] A Desperate Prayer Answered at the Top of the World, *Guideposts*, 2011-11-15, accessed 2019-03-16.

[30] Speakman, *Four Season*, 75.

[31] Ibid., 187.

[32] Center for Substance Abuse Treatment. Enhancing Motivation for Change in Substance Abuse Treatment. Treatment Improvement

Protocol (TIP) Series, No. 35. HHS Publication No. (SMA) 13-4212. Rockville, Maryland: Substance Abuse and Mental Health Services Administration, 1999, 17.

[33] PAL (parents of addicted loved ones), Lesson #2, the "Three Promises to a Loved-one Suffering from Addiction," June 2017, palgroup.org.

[34] PAL (parents of addicted loved ones), Gems handout, June 2017.

[35] PAL, "Unhealthy vs. Healthy."

[36] Ibid.

[37] Melody Beattie, *The Language of Letting Go* (Hazelden foundation, 1990).

[38] PAL, Gems handout.

[39] Quote from "As Bill See's It," Fourth Edition of Alcoholics Anonymous Press, November 2001, 115.

[40] PAL (parents of addicted loved -ones), Lesson quote, Supplemental Lesson, "Respond Rather than React," palgroup.org, June 2017.

[41] Charles R. Swindoll, *The Grace Awakening* (Dallas: Word, 1990), 146–47.

[42] M. Scott Peck, *Further along the Road Less Traveled: the Unending Journey toward Spiritual Growth: The Edited Lectures* (New York: Simon & Schuster, 1993), 46.

About the Author

Mary Allyson was born and raised in Washington. She has a BA in ministry leadership. After retiring as COO from a multimillion-dollar business, she earned a master's degree in substance abuse and passed the state board examination for her license, enabling her to work in a large Christian treatment center, where she worked as an addiction therapist in detox, residential, partial hospitalization, and intensive outpatient.

Addiction has always been part of Mary's life. First, she grew up with a step-grandfather and uncle who were alcoholics. Secondly, she married an alcoholic, eventually divorcing him after ten years of marriage, thinking she could put alcoholism out of her life forever. Little did she know that alcoholism could be genetically passed onto her children. As a parent of three alcoholic daughters, she did what most parents do in trying to fix their children's problems caused by alcoholism. She became the worst kind of enabler. At this point, she committed herself to change, attending weekly Al-Anon meetings.

In March 2015, she and several other parents launched the grassroots nonprofit organization, PAL (parents of addicted loved ones), originally founded by Mike Speakman. PAL has meetings in most states, with demand for more coming in every day (palgroup.org). Besides being on the PAL board of directors, she facilitates a weekly national phone conference meetings where parents/family members with addicted adult children call in for help, support, and education on the lessons that Speakman created. She has worked with hundreds of parents trying to deal with the sorrow and pain caused from having an adult child addicted to alcohol/drugs.